CAREERS GUIDE

What Do I Want To Be?

A Guided Journal to Help You Discover Your Passion

By Leigh St John

ISBN: 1441422978 and EAN-13: 9781441422972

Publish the Dream!

The Passion is spreading...

What others are saying:

"I know I'm only in high school but ...your book... helped me know that I have lots of choices but only some of them are what I want to do with my life because only some of them are my passion. My family don't have a lot but they want me to be happy. I didn't think I could ever go to law school because I didn't think we could afford it so like it says in your book I didn't let myself want that. Now I know there is always a way even if it might take me longer. I do want to go to law school and now I believe I can." *Brittany, Student*

"You inspire the students in a way very few people can. As a teacher who passionately cares about them, thank you!" *Cheryl Burns, Masters in Education, Administration and Supervision*

"Thank you for letting me have an advance copy of your book. I'm one of those people who have too many passions. I used to feel totally overwhelmed because I love to do many different things. Your book helped me find that there was a single core passion in the middle of it all and I am now clear on what I want to study. Thank you for bringing me out of my overwhelmnedness." *Maricel, College Student*

"I would love to say I have read your book, but I took it home and haven't seen it since! My son borrowed it and loved it, so when he was finished with it he loaned it to his girlfriend, who loved it so much she asked if she could loan it to her sister, who has since loaned it to a young girl she is mentoring.

What I can say is thank you for writing a book that transcends age, status, occupation, and for giving me the gift of a totally transformed son. I am yet to learn what he learned in your book but he is a different young man as a result. For the first time he is focused and happy and I thank you. Whatever you wrote in your book really reached him in a way that no one else has been able to." *Clara West, Mother of three*

"Leigh, this wonderful book is a shining light and constant inspiration. Thank you for your gifts from the heart. You have touched more lives than you will ever know!" *Liza Foster, Managing Director of Soul Direction*

"Congratulations! Your powerful awakening to passion as the guiding light in your life is inspirational, ... brilliant in fact!" *Samantha Backman, CEO of health researcher, Revivalife*

The Passion is spreading...

"Congratulations on ... the publication of (Discovering Your Passion). As a single operator you are so far ahead of many who for years struggle to make a difference.

It is obvious to me that you have a clearly defined model for success, and in particular apply that to your own personal development and your journey, which I can only imagine on many occasions is quite challenging. Many thanks and congratulations!" *John Braithwaite, Development Manager, King's College*

"Passion for life is everything and you are to be applauded for creating the pointy end of the experience!" *Bonnie Sleep - Bond University School of Business Lecturer*

"You truly are an inspiration to people who want to aspire to excellence...and you have taught me that I have the answers to my own questions." *Bindy Marshall, Bose*

"I knew once I picked up your book and before I finished the acknowledgements that my life had turned a corner because my husband and I had been struggling with what we wanted ideally and our reality of living in suburban rat race hell. We both so desperately wanted to make fundamental changes to our lives and yet lacked the road map of questions that we needed to ask ourselves. Yes we both have read seemingly all the motivational books out there however it wasn't enough, they tend to pump you up to take a few steps and then the hot air flows out of your momentum. I know it is our low self esteem and letting our disappointments overwhelm us, we have tried, I have tried and I know, I know, I know!

Then I picked up your book and boom, its not about telling me how I have a negative attitude, it is asking me to clean out the clutter, so I go and have a garage sale, take a whole heap of rubbish to the dump and my negative attitude goes with it! Now, how about those books that tell me that my disappointments are overwhelming me? No your book asks me to write down all my successes for each day and boom, no more over whelming disappointments.

Smell the sweetness of success because I know that you haven't done all this work for fame and fortune. Your inner light has wanted to help people who have struggled like you and you have shared your journey to empower us. With heartfelt gratitude I thank you for writing your book. And enjoy feeling all the positive energy pouring back to you from those of us who are reading your book and 'getting it'." *Rochelle Ryan-Bax, Creative Memories*

A note from the Author, Leigh St John:

You will notice that those whose testimonials appear in this book are not all high-profile "celebrities" as is the case with the vast majority of books.

Although I have many well-known people to whom I could have turned for their thoughts on this Journal, I decided to go with the reflections from "every-day" people, students, teachers…

This book is written for students just like you – it is written for *you* to help you find *your* place, *your* purpose, *your* passion.

"Put yourself in a state of mind where you say to yourself, "Here is an opportunity for me to celebrate like never before, my own power, my own ability to get myself to do whatever is necessary."
Anthony Robbins

This book is dedicated to my
great-grandmother.

Nan, you were and always will be
my role model,
my guiding light and
my inspiration to be the best I can be.

"With every [one] I love who has been taken into the brown bosom of the earth a part of me has been buried there; but their contribution to my being of happiness, strength and understanding remains to sustain me in an altered world." Helen Keller

---

What do I want to be?

A Self-Discovery Guided Journal

"A man (or woman) is a success if he gets up in the morning and goes to bed at night and in between does what he wants to do." Bob Dylan

What if you could be doing anything in the world that you wanted to be doing... What would that be? If there were no limitations... If money was not an obstacle... If education was not an obstacle... If family obligations were not an obstacle... What would your life look like?

"What do I want to be?" provides a thirteen-week program that guides you from where you are through the journey of discovering your passion and realizing your potential.

Rather than 'telling' you what you should or could be doing with your life, **"What do I want to be?"** provides you with the basic tools and then challenges you with a series of exercises and questions to help you **understand** and then **embrace** the **power of passion.**

"Twenty years from now you will be more disappointed by the things you didn't do than by the ones you did do. So throw off the bowlines. Sail away from the safe harbor. Catch the trade winds in your sails. Explore. Dream. Discover." Mark Twain

"I can teach anybody how to get what they want out of life. The problem is that I can't find anybody who can tell me what they want." Mark Twain

"What do I want to be?" will show you how to:

- Explore your life's purpose
- Gain new confidence in your own creative powers
- Discover the power of focus
- Clear the clutter in your life
- Ask better questions to get better answers
- Dissolve self-limiting thought patterns
- Turn your aspirations into reality and
- Live the life of your dreams!

Whether you have a vague idea of your passion or no idea at all, **"What do I want to be?"** will work with you through the process of not only discovering your passion, but also putting into practice the steps necessary to actually live your passion.

- What if you really could start your own business..?
- What if you really could become a doctor, lawyer, psychologist..?
- What if you really could teach English in China..?

You can do it! All you have to do is take the journey. *Ready..?*

"When the heart is ignored or suppressed, the result is the same for the organization as it is for the individual: unrealized potential." Richard Chang, 'The Passion Plan at Work'

Contents

Introduction

"Our deepest fear is not that we are inadequate.

Our deepest fear is that we are powerful beyond measure. It is our light, not our darkness that most frightens us.

We ask ourselves, Who am I to be brilliant, gorgeous, talented, fabulous? Actually, who are you not to be?

You are a child of God. Your playing small does not serve the world. There is nothing enlightened about shrinking so that other people won't feel insecure around you.

We are all meant to shine, as children do. We are born to make manifest the glory of God that is within us. It's not just in some of us, it's in everyone.

And as we let our own light shine, we unconsciously give other people permission to do the same. As we are liberated from our own fears, our presence automatically liberates others."

Marianne Williamson from A Return To Love:
Reflections on the Principles of A Course in Miracles

Let's start at the very beginning…

Congratulations!!! You'd be surprised how many adults have no idea what they want to do with their life – and in many cases, their life is more than half over! Yours is just beginning – and through this book we will work together to help you discover what you are passionate about and what you want to be!

So many people talk about not being able to discover their passion and that's as far as they get. You have actually done something about it by at least starting to read this book.

Now, continue the journey, read the book, do the activities – you never know where it may take you…

How This Book Came To Be Written

"A rock pile ceases to be a rock pile the moment a single man contemplates it, bearing within him the image of a cathedral." Antoine De Saint-Exupery

- ❑ **What is my ultimate purpose?**
- ❑ **What should I study?**
- ❑ **Why am I here?**
- ❑ **What is the meaning of my life?**
- ❑ **How do I get past all the clutter?**
- ❑ **What is my passion?**

These were the questions that I was hearing over and over again from people in different cities, in different countries…

Then, someone said, "you should write a book on this", and this book is the result.

I know what it's like not to know what you want to be, what you want to study, what you want to do with your life. That's how I also knew the questions to ask you to help you find your own answers.

"I went to the woods because I wished to live deliberately, to front only the essential facts of life, and see if I could not learn what it had to teach, and not, when I came to die, discover that I had not lived." Henry David Thoreau

What You Will Find In This Book...

Although you could simply sit down and read the book through, it is designed as a '**workbook**'. You are encouraged to carry out each of the activities and answer each of the questions. It is also designed as a **journal**. There are spaces for you to write your responses, your thoughts and even doodle and draw if that is what you need to do in order to tap into that part of your brain that is hiding your passion from view.

You will also find a series of **quotations** from other inspirational people. If you would like to access these quotes and others, you can view them by going to www.LeighStJohn.com.

You will find that this book is about more than just discovering your passion and working out what you want to be. It is focused on helping you to realize your potential and be the best <u>you</u> that you can be.

You will learn to let go of the past, reward yourself for your achievements, acknowledge your strengths and develop a belief that you really can achieve anything to which you set your mind – and don't worry if you are like many students and you are not sure what you are good at – we'll guide you through that process.

"Finish every day and be done with it. You have done what you could. Some blunders and absurdities no doubt have crept in; forget them as soon as you can. Tomorrow is a new day; begin it well and serenely and with too high a spirit to be cumbered with your old nonsense. This day is all that is good and fair. It is too dear, with its hopes and invitations, to waste a moment on yesterdays." Ralph Waldo Emerson

Keeping A Journal

"Journal writing is a voyage to the interior." Christina Baldwin

If you are like many people (myself included once upon a time), the thought or writing in a book makes your stomach churn. If you are one of these people, I suggest you purchase a separate Journal in which to write.

"I... recommend to every one of my Readers, the keeping a Journal of their Lives for one Week, and setting down punctually their whole Series of Employments during that Space of Time. This kind of Self-Examination would give them a true State of themselves, and incline them to consider seriously what they are about. One Day would rectifie the Omissions of another, and make a Man weigh all those indifferent Actions, which, though they are easily forgotten, must certainly be accounted for."
Joseph Addison, 1712

Keeping a journal is also beneficial in that it gives you a place where you can pour out your thoughts knowing that the only person who is going to see them is you – unless you decide to share them, of course.

"Arranging a bowl of flowers in the morning can give a sense of quiet in a crowded day - like writing a poem, or saying a prayer."
Anne Morrow Lindbergh

There Is No One Right Answer

So often we are taught to find THE answer. In your math class, I'm fairly certain that the teacher expects you to give THE right answer, not necessarily provide a series of POSSIBLE answers.

In this book, there is no ONE right answer – there may be several.

If you love teaching, travel, skydiving and writing, don't think for a minute that this book is going to suggest that you have to pick ONE right answer, ONE passion.

What if you could do them all?

What if you could travel the world teaching skydiving and writing about it for magazines?

As you progress through this book, challenge yourself (and your partner if you are working with one) to not stop when you get *one* answer. Keep going. Come up with as many answers as you can. The first five or six may be good – and the seventh may be great!

"Do you remember how electrical currents and "unseen waves" were laughed at? The knowledge about man is still in its infancy." Albert Einstein

The Answers Are In You

Have you ever heard of Socrates? He was a classical Greek philosopher who believed that we all have the answers inside us when it comes to things like knowing what we want to be – we just need to have the right questions.

"The thing always happens that you really believe in; and the belief in a thing makes it happen." Frank Lloyd Wright

This is the style I have chosen to use in this book.

"The simplest questions are the most profound. Where were you born? Where is your home? Where are you going? What are you doing? Think about these once in a while and watch your answers change." Richard Bach

Your journey through this book will be signposted with a variety of questions, challenges, activities and exercises, all geared toward you finding the answers within you.

"To the question of your life you are the answer, and to the problems of your life you are the solution." Joe Cordare

Questions, Exercises, Action Items

"Don't ask yourself what the world needs; ask yourself what makes you come alive. And then go and do that. Because what the world needs is people who have come alive." Dr Howard Thurman

Throughout the book you will see the following:

Consider...

and

Your Thoughts...

This is when you will be asked to consider a question, do an exercise, take action on a particular topic or simply note your thoughts on the subject. This will help you along the way to working out what you want to be.

I encourage you to not just 'read' the questions and exercises but to actually 'do' each one.

"All that we are is the result of what we have thought. The mind is everything. What we think, we become." Maharishi Mahesh Yogi

Working With A Partner

"Nothing average ever stood as a monument to progress. When progress is looking for a partner it doesn't turn to those who believe they are only average. It turns instead to those who are forever searching and striving to become the best they possibly can. If we seek the average level we cannot hope to achieve a high level of success." A. Lou Vickery

Although everyone is different and learns in different ways, I would suggest that you at least consider working with a partner through this book.

The benefits are:

❑ You feel as though you are not alone
❑ You have someone with whom to bounce ideas
❑ You have someone to challenge you
❑ You have someone to talk with who understands (they are going through the same process)

How To Work With A Partner

There are many ways that you and your partner could work through this program together. Here is just one suggestion:

1. Each of you reads through the chapter separately
2. You get together in person, on the telephone, online – whatever means works best for you
3. You discuss your thoughts about the chapter in general
4. You discuss the questions and suggested actions, what they mean to you, what ideas you have and ask any questions you many have
5. You set a time to get together again to discuss your responses to the action items
6. Each of you then separately completes the questions and actions
7. You get together again to discuss your responses and to challenge and support one another.

Then you start the whole process over again for the next chapter.

"I believe that [everyone] is the keeper of a dream - and by tuning into one another's secret hopes, we can become better friends, better partners, better parents, and better lovers."
Oprah Winfrey, O Magazine, June 2003

Consider...

- ❑ If you were to work with a partner, who would you choose?

- ❑ Why?

- ❑ Are you going to ask them?

- ❑ If not, why not?

Can One Person Make A Difference?

"You must be the change you wish to see in the world."
Mahatma Ghandi

People sometimes have amazingly large and seemingly unachievable dreams and goals and I am often asked whether one person really can make a difference.

I would like to share a story with you from Loren Eisley's book, "The Star Thrower". The story goes a little like this:-

A man who had been walking along a beach saw a boy throwing starfish into the ocean in an attempt to save them from the heat of the rising sun. The older man made a comment that, because of the number of starfish, the boy couldn't possibly make a difference, to which the boy replied as he threw yet another starfish into the ocean and past the breaking waves, "It made a difference to that one."

By the way, I would thoroughly recommend Eisley's books. He has a way of looking at things we often take for granted in a totally different way.

"You can make a difference with your everyday actions. Listen to the stories told around our planet, and you will hear this message over and over again." Tony Ryan, Author of "The Ripple Effect"

Your Thoughts…

Are You A Yebbit?

Are you a member of the Yebbit Family? Yebbit = Yeah, But...

"Happy are those who dream dreams and are ready to pay the price to make them come true." Leon J. Suenes

When asked about following or pursuing your dreams, goals and passions, have you said, "yeah, but there is this to take care of."

"Yeah, but I have to look after such and such first."

"Yeah, but I'll do it when I graduate."

"Yeah, but it takes time that I just don't have."

Yeah, but – yeah, but – yebbit, yebbit, yebbit..!

"To be always intending to make a new and better life but never to find time to set about it is as...to put off eating and drinking and sleeping from one day to the next until you're dead." Og Mandino

Consider...

❑   When have you been a part of the Yebbit Family?

❑   What were you trying to avoid? Why?

What Are You Waiting For?

"The future depends on what we do in the present." Mahatma
Gandhi

Many years ago I enrolled in a college program and, because I allowed 'life' to get in the way, I ended up deferring and then, because I felt that it would take too long to achieve, I finally withdrew.

I had always thought about how long it would take, particularly part-time, to achieve that degree and it seemed like 'forever'!

Well, some years later I moved house and in the unpacking discovered a box of old papers. In amongst those old papers were my original enrolment forms with the expected dates of completion.

You guessed it.

The expected date of completion of that degree - that I stopped working toward because it would take too long - had already passed some months ago.

Had I continued on that path that seemed never-ending, I would have completed that particular journey, with all the experiences, knowledge and piece of paper that came with it.

Yes, things do get in the way, but only if you let them.

We all have the same amount of time in a day – what you do with yours is up to you.

Consider...

- ❑ How much time do you spend thinking about your problems? How much time do you spend thinking about your dreams?

- ❑ Reflect on your answer to the above question when you look at how much time you spend on your problems as opposed to how much time you spend on fulfilling your dreams. What's really more important?

Consider...

"Focus 90% of your time on solutions and only 10% of your time on problems." Anthony J. D'Angelo, The College Blue Book

❑   Why have you chosen to allocate your time accordingly?

❑   What could you do differently from now on?

Your Thoughts...

Is This New?

"If you resist reading what you disagree with, how will you ever acquire deeper insights into what you believe? The things most worth reading are precisely those that challenge our convictions." Author Unknown

This book almost wasn't written in that I just couldn't get past the hurdle in my own mind that very little if anything in the area of careers resources is "new", and I didn't want to simply re-do what was already out there.

Where I hope this book – this Journal – is able to inspire you to discover your passion and to be the best you can be, is through the use of questions to help you find **the answers that are within you**.

I encourage you to read as much as you can from a variety of authors and take on board anything that 'feels' right.

Remember, the answers are already within you – the job of this journal is simply to help you find them.

"You may be disappointed if you fail, but you are doomed if you don't try." Beverly Sills

Your Thoughts...

The Past Does Not Equal The Future

> *"If history is any guide, much of what we take for granted simply isn't true."* John Hagelin, PhD, *"What the Bleep Do We Know"*

Consider these changing beliefs:

- ❑ The Earth was believed to be flat – now it's round.

- ❑ The Earth was believed to be the center of the Solar System – now it's the Sun.

Consider the four-minute mile. It was once thought to be the physical limit of the human body.

On May 6, 1954, Englishman Roger Bannister ran the first sub-four-minute mile in recorded history at 3 minutes 59.4 seconds. Six weeks later, Australian John Landy, followed suit with a run of 3 minutes and 58 seconds. Now it's the standard of all professional middle distance runners.

- ❑ The four-minute mile was impossible – now it's a standard.

> *"It [Avon] all started back in 1886 when the company's founder, an entrepreneur named David McConnell, recruited women to sell perfume door-to-door. This was considered quite revolutionary at the time because women virtually never worked outside the home and would not win the right to vote for another 34 years."* Andrea Jung Chairman and CEO, Avon Products Inc, as quoted in *"Avon, Building the World's Premier Company for Women"* by Laura Klepacki

Consider...

"Nothing is predestined: The obstacles of your past can become the gateways that lead to new beginnings." Ralph Blum

❑   What beliefs do you have about your past that are not necessarily true for your present or your future? For example, was there a time when you found something difficult that, if you tried it again now, might not seem so hard?

❑   Why have you held onto those beliefs?

❑   What habits do you feel are trapping you?

❑   What could you do about them?

Your Thoughts...

Part 1: Understanding The Power

"The man who views the world at fifty the same as he did at twenty has wasted thirty years of his life."
Muhammad Ali

"No one can make you feel inferior without your consent." *Eleanor Roosevelt*

Before you can even *begin* to work out your passion or passions, you need to understand three basic questions –

1. Who you are
2. Where you are and
3. Why you are there

Throughout the six weeks of Part 1, you will begin to understand the power of just how special you really are; how your thoughts and attitudes can have an enormous impact on your ability to discover and achieve your passions; and how you can clear the way to fully realize your potential.

"If you have built castles in the air, your work need not be lost; that is where they should be. Now put foundations under them."
Henry David Thoreau

Along the way you will experience many challenges and be asked to review your existing thoughts and opinions on a variety of subjects.

"I am not discouraged because every wrong attempt discarded is a step forward." Thomas Edison

---

Some people will be tempted to skip this Part and move straight to Part 2. I encourage you to work your way through this journal, completing Part 1 first.

You will have heard of the statement about not being able to see the forest for the trees, yes?

Well, that's exactly what this is. You need to work through the clutter and adjust your viewpoint so that you can discover your *true* passion, not merely the one that *seems* right at the time.

"Assume that whatever situation you are facing at the moment is exactly the right situation you need to ultimately be successful. This situation has been sent to help you become better, to help you expand and grow." Brian Tracy

---

Consider...

- Be alert for times when you may encounter ideas in this book that promote strong negative reactions within you. For example: Think about when you are asked to consider that no one can make you feel inferior – or any other emotion – and that you and you alone decide how you will feel. If this statement produces a reaction in you that is one of, "that's ridiculous! Of course people can make me feel angry and upset!" then consider the following:

- Just suppose for a moment that Eleanor Roosevelt was right (you will find her quote again in "Every Conscious Action is a Choice").

- What if the only person who can make you feel inferior is you?

- How could that idea have an impact on your life?

As you proceed through this book, I ask you to suspend your judgment and be on the lookout for any time you have a strong negative reaction. You may just have hit a nerve within you that needs to be healed before you can discover and then live your passion!

What Is 'Passion'?

"Nothing great was ever achieved without enthusiasm." Ralph
Waldo Emerson

According to several dictionaries, passion is described as:

- ❏   A powerful emotion
- ❏   An ardent love
- ❏   Boundless enthusiasm

To me, your 'passion' is whatever provides that feeling inside where you just
can't wait to get into it. It's when your eyes light up talking about it. It's
whatever makes you glow. It's the thing that makes you come alive.

"It's kind of fun to do the impossible." Walt Disney

Many people have never experienced that feeling – or if they have, they have
forgotten what brought it about in the first place.

If that's you, relax. You are in good company.

Even the vast majority of adults with whom I have worked over the years have
no idea what their passion is and when challenged to find the thing or things
that make them come alive, draw a blank.

The first part of this book, Understanding the Power, will take you through a
series of exercises, week by week, to help you clear the clutter that may be in
the way of you seeing what your passion truly is.

*"When one door closes another opens. But often we look so long
so regretfully upon the closed door that we fail to see the one that
has opened for us."* Alexander Graham Bell

Before you can truly know your passion, you need to be in a place:

- ❑ Where you can honestly acknowledge that you deserve to live your dreams;
- ❑ Where you are not self-sabotaging your efforts;
- ❑ Where you have adjusted your attitudes;
- ❑ Where you are accepting others for who they are;
- ❑ Where you realize that everything has energy and
- ❑ Where you truly understand that every conscious action is a choice and your choices have lead you to where you are right now.

Each of those elements is covered in this first section of **"What do I want to be?"**.

"The ancient Greek definition of happiness was the full use of your powers along lines of excellence." John F. Kennedy

---

Your Thoughts...

The Power Of Motivation

"All our dreams can come true - if we have the courage to pursue them." Walt Disney

Imagine you have just received notification that you have won five million dollars!

All you need do to collect your money is, in ten days time, go to the bank and sign a document so that your signature matches the one that the school or college has on file. If you cannot do this, you forfeit the money.

Easy, right?

For the first five days you are jumping around with unrestrained glee thinking about what you will do with the money. Then, unexpectedly, you have an accident and break your right arm.

The doctor puts it in a cast and advises you that it will be at least two or three weeks before you will be able to use your fingers.

Dilemma! You are right-handed and need to sign for your money in only five days.

"It is not because things are difficult that we do not dare, it is because we do not dare that they are difficult." Seneca

Not one to be deterred, you begin practicing signing your name with your left hand until, just hours before the deadline, you get your left-handed signature to look just like your right-handed signature.

You have your money and everyone is happy.

"Success is the good fortune that comes from aspiration, desperation, perspiration and inspiration." Evan Esar

❑ What was it that motivated you to try so hard?

❑ Would you have tried that hard to overcome your obstacle if it weren't for the money?

❑ Consider how many times in your life you have failed to be inspired enough and motivated enough to take the action needed.

You can change your future by changing your present. Make today the day you start being inspired enough to take the actions that will lead you realizing your full potential.

"There is no such thing in anyone's life as an unimportant day."
Alexander Woollcott

Consider...

❑ Consider the role of motivation in the above story.

❑ What was it that made you work so incredibly hard to achieve your objective?

❑ How could you tap into that next time you wanted to achieve something?

Your Thoughts...

Week 1: Getting Ready - Clearing The Clutter

"Out of clutter, find simplicity." Albert Einstein

Clearing the clutter in your life can do amazing things for your clarity as well as make room for what you want in your life to appear.

Your mission this week is to clear what is commonly referred to as "baggage":

- ❏ Forgive yourself
- ❏ Literally clean up your life
- ❏ Resolve old 'business'
- ❏ Learn that "no" can be a complete sentence
- ❏ Take care of your needs

Before you can begin to discover your passion, you need to clear the clutter so that you can see your way forward.

Forgive Yourself

Why is it that so many people can forgive others more easily and readily than they can forgive themselves?

The first thing we need to be clear on here is that forgiveness is not the same as condoning. Just because you forgive, doesn't mean you say that what was done was "ok".

Forgiveness is an acknowledgement that we are all human and we all make mistakes.

"Anyone who has never made a mistake has never tried anything new." Albert Einstein

The second thing we need to be clear on is the pay off we get for *not* forgiving ourselves.

Pay off? How could there possibly be a pay off for feeling so rotten and not forgiving ourselves – or others – for what may have been done?

The pain, anger, resentment and other emotions we feel when we have done something 'wrong' – or if we feel someone has done something wrong to us – are a very successful barrier against being hurt again.

So how do we forgive ourselves?

Your Thoughts…

Consider...

- ❑ Think of a situation where you have done something you consider being 'wrong'. For example: It could be that you did or said something hurtful that had serious consequences. It could be that you acted illegally. It could be that you lied to someone. Whatever it is, choose one situation.

- ❑ Write down what you did.

Consider…

❏ Write down why you did it – and try to go a little deeper than just what might seem obvious to you at the time.

❏ Write down what you were trying to achieve.

❏ Now, consider your answers.

❏ Did you intend to cause the problem(s) you caused?

❏ Did you intend to hurt people or yourself?

Whatever your answers, consider that you did the best you could at the time, given the situation, given your life experiences to date, given your knowledge at the time – and because you did the best you could at the time, you deserve to be forgiven by you.

Consider...

- ❏ Write out the following statements on a separate sheet of paper:

- ❏ I made a mistake
- ❏ I am human
- ❏ I can't change the past
- ❏ I am sorry for my actions
- ❏ I forgive myself

- ❏ Now, read those statements aloud from your own handwriting.

...and then read them aloud again.

Keep reading them aloud until it "feels" right. By that I mean, the first time you read them it may feel as though you are lying to yourself, with your inner dialogue being something like, "I'll say it but I don't really believe it."

Keep reading the statements over and over until you feel a sense of release and acceptance. That's what forgiveness feels like: release; acceptance; like a weight has just been lifted; like you have been set free.

It is your choice to forgive yourself or not – but you can't truly live your passion if you are carrying the burden of guilt with you every day.

Your Thoughts...

Literally Clean Up Your Life

Look around you – what do you see?

- ❏ Is your bedroom overrun with 'stuff'?
- ❏ Is your wardrobe full of clothes you haven't worn in ages?
- ❏ Is your life full of people who no longer share the same interests or things that are important to you?
- ❏ Are you still obsessing over a past boyfriend/girlfriend?

There is a saying that "nature abhors a vacuum". In other words, you need to clear space if you want something new and wonderful to come and fill it.

Consider...

- ❑ Consider the elements of your life that need to be un-cluttered:

  - o Home
  - o Study
  - o Friends/Family
  - o Financial
  - o Spiritual

Now complete the following:

- ❑ Write a list of as many things as you can that you would like to un-clutter in your life.

Consider...

- ❑ Sort through that list and come up with the top 13 you feel are most significant.

1.	
2.	
3.	
4.	
5.	
6.	
7.	
8.	
9.	
10.	
11.	
12.	
13.	

- ❑ Schedule one task per week for the next thirteen weeks of this journey – starting with one task THIS WEEK!

Remember, they do not need to be earth-shatteringly difficult. Just cleaning up your room may be a simple one (although I haven't seen the state of your room – maybe that task's not so simple!)

- ❑ Start one of them **NOW!**

Resolve 'Old Business'

Part of clearing clutter is resolving old business.

You know, the things that you should have, could have, would have…

"In the middle of difficulty lies opportunity." Albert Einstein

In my case, when I did this exercise, I listed things such as –

- ❑ People with whom I had lost touch that I wanted to look up
- ❑ Thank you notes I wanted to send but hadn't
- ❑ Projects I had started but not made the time to complete that I really wanted to complete
- ❑ Photos I wanted to put into an album

"All glory comes from daring to begin." William Shakespeare

Consider…

- ❑ Consider the elements in your life that you would consider to be 'old business'.

- ❑ Make a list of anything that you would like to resolve, fix, take care of…

- ❑ For each one, note why you want to take care of it.

Consider...

□   Choose 13 items from the list that you would like to tackle first.

1.	
2.	
3.	
4.	
5.	
6.	
7.	
8.	
9.	
10.	
11.	
12.	
13.	

□   Schedule one item per week for the next thirteen weeks, starting with one THIS WEEK!

Just as with the last section, they do not need to be huge assignments. One could simply be to send five thank you notes that you had wanted to send. Whatever you choose is up to you.

□   Now, look at the one you have scheduled for this week and start it **IMMEDIATELY!**

Learn That "No" Can Be A Complete Sentence

Before you can discover and live your passion, you need to make sure that the things in your life are the ones to which you want to say, "yes".

"I've learned that you shouldn't go through life with a catcher's mitt on both hands; you need to be able to throw some things back." Maya Angelou

---

We so often get caught up in trying to explain why we have elected not to do something that we end up doing it anyway.

While I'm not talking about saying "no" to your parents, I'd like you to think about how many times you have been asked to help out somewhere, for instance. Now think about the times when, by helping out, you would be letting yourself down or not fulfilling other promises you may have made.

You try to explain why you need to say "no" and then magically part way through your very detailed explanation, you find yourself saying, "OK".

While it is good manners to be courteous in your decline, it is important to be equally able to simply say, "no, thank you". Period, end of story.

One thing of which we do need to be aware, however, is that we teach people how to treat us and if we have been saying "yes" all this time, people will expect us to continue to say "yes".

So, what happens when we say "no"? They will be confused, bewildered, and possibly offended.

Should this persuade you to say, "yes" all the time? NO!

The reason for providing this insight is to make you aware of the challenge you will be facing and the responses you may receive.

Remember, if you have taught them to expect you to say, "yes" all the time, you can teach them to expect you to say, "no" sometimes.

It's all a matter of being true to yourself so that you can be true to others.

Besides, if you are saying "yes" all the time in an effort not to hurt anyone's feelings, soon you will reach a point – if you haven't already – where you have so much on your plate that you can't keep your promises and then you end up hurting their feelings anyway.

"I don't know the key to success but the key to failure is trying to please everybody." Bill Cosby

Consider...

- ❏ Think about something to which you would like to be able to say "no".

- ❏ Why would you like to say "no"?

- ❏ Visualize in your mind being asked.

Consider...

- Now imagine yourself simply saying, "no, thank you." How do you feel?

- If you feel uncomfortable, what could you tell yourself to make yourself feel more at ease with saying "no"? Remember, you are looking after *you* so you are better able to serve others.

- In most instances, that won't be the end of it. So, imagine the entire conversation back and forth with you holding your ground, not going into an elaborate explanation, and simply repeating that in this instance the answer is "no" but thanking them anyway.

You might even like to practice with a friend or partner and have them be the other person – and make sure they are not too easy on you!

This is a hard skill to master but one that will serve you well.

Your Thoughts...

Week 2: Adjusting Attitudes

"Everything that people create is a projection of what's inside them." Stuart Lichtman

Life is based on decisions – attitudes lead to decisions – better attitudes, better decisions.

This week we are going to take a look at attitudes – not "bad attitudes" or "good attitudes" but attitude in general and how a shift in your attitude can have an impact on discovering your passion and realizing your potential.

"By the way that we think and by the way that we believe in things, in that way our world is created." Pema Chodron

In particular we will discuss the following:

- ❑ Build your confidence and self-esteem.
- ❑ We all have filters.
- ❑ You control your emotions.
- ❑ FEAR – False Evidence Appearing Real.
- ❑ You are an amazing individual.
- ❑ You deserve the very best.
- ❑ Who are you?
- ❑ It's ok to say "I am good at this!"

"An optimist sees an opportunity in every calamity; a pessimist sees a calamity in every opportunity." Winston Churchill

"The longer I live, the more I realize the impact of attitude on life.

Attitude to me is more important than facts. It is more important than the past, than education, than money, than circumstances, than failures, than success, than what other people think or say or do. It is more important than appearance, gift, or skill. It will make or break a company...a church...a home.

The remarkable thing is we have a choice every day regarding the attitude we will embrace for that day. We cannot change our past...we cannot change the fact that people will act in a certain way.

We cannot change the inevitable. The only thing we can do is play on the string we have, and that is our attitude.

I am convinced that life is 10 percent what happens to me and 90 percent how I react to it. And so it is with you... we are in charge of our attitudes." Charles Swindoll

Step 1 – Build Your Confidence And Self-Esteem

"The future belongs to those who believe in the beauty of their dreams." Eleanor Roosevelt

Before you can hope to effectively alter your attitude to one of tolerance, understanding and the expectation of great things, you need to ensure that your confidence and self-esteem are strong.

"Quality begins on the inside... and then works its way out." Bob Moawad

Why aren't we as confident as we would like to be?

Why have we chosen to listen to the people who put us down and tell us "it can't be done" or "you're not good enough"?

"Pay no attention to what the critics say; no statue has ever been erected to a critic." Jean Sibelius, Finnish Composer

Consider...

❏ For the next three days, keep this journal with you and write down EVERY success you have – no matter how large or how small.

These could be successes such as:

❏ You arrived to school/college on time.
❏ You cooked a great steak (something I would love to master!)
❏ You were there for a friend who needed you.
❏ You successfully completed the project that you have been working on for a long time.
❏ You exercised every day.
❏ You took time out to paint.

Even if you think they are minor or trivial, list them.

❏ At the end of the three days, review your list.

❏ Choose the most significant success you had and celebrate that success.

❏ Do this activity every week for the remainder of this program (and even longer if you like).

Your Thoughts...

Day 1... My Successes

Day 2... My Successes

Day 3... My Successes

We All Have Filters

"If in the last few years you haven't discarded a major opinion or acquired a new one, check your pulse. You may be dead." Gelett Burgess

What are 'filters'? They are the result of life experiences. They are the feelings, emotions and information that change the way we see what we see.

For example, if I say, "think of a car". Chances are you will be thinking of a different type, make, model and color car than the one in my mind.

Why?

Chances are we have different cars in our respective garages. We have friends who drive different cars from one another and so on.

"There are only two ways to live your life. One is as though nothing is a miracle. The other is as though everything is a miracle." Albert Einstein

I was teaching a retail course many years ago and was trying to explain the subject of filters to my class. Unbeknown to my group, I had pre-arranged with a colleague to come in at a particular time, speak with me for a moment, hang around the desk area and then leave.

About ten minutes after he left, I said to the class, "just suppose I said to you that I have discovered my wallet is missing and the only person other than myself who had access to it was the person to whom I was just speaking. Can you give me a description of that person?"

The responses were that he (at least they got that bit right!) was about 5'11" down to 5'6", he had brown hair, blonde hair or dark brown hair, he was wearing a dark shirt, a light shirt, plain shirt, with stripes, dark pants, light pants – and they all agreed he was wearing shoes although what color they were was open for debate as well.

The interesting thing was that everyone was relatively sure they were right. Just about everyone's response differed in some way from the others, however they all held reasonably firmly to the fact that their recollection was correct.

At the completion of the activity, I asked my colleague to come back into the class and funnily enough, not one of the participants was able to get the height, hair color and clothing color all correct.

What does this activity tell us?

So often we hear things or see things and then make decisions based on what we 'think' we see or hear.

"Sometimes I've believed as many as six impossible things before breakfast." Lewis Carroll

How many times have you heard two people recount the same event and it sounds like two separate events? The song from the classic movie *'Gigi'*, "Ah yes, I remember it well," is a good example.

"We met at nine – we met at eight; I was on time – no you were late…"

Why is it important to recognize our filters?

"It is only when we silent the blaring sounds of our daily existence that we can finally hear the whispers of truth that life reveals to us, as it stands knocking on the doorsteps of our hearts" K.T. Jong

When clearing the way to discover your passion, you need to be open to new ideas, new ways of thinking and new opportunities. When we do not acknowledge our filters and rigidly hold on to what we 'believe' to be the way things are, we are clouding our judgment.

Remember, people once believed the Earth was flat and as such, until someone was open enough to challenge that belief – to challenge those filters – there was no possibility of ever sailing around the globe and discovering lands on the other side of the world (because if you asked them, there *was* no other side of the world!).

"The first and most important step toward…success is the feeling that we can succeed." Nelson Boswell

Communicating with others

When communicating with others, in addition to our filters, consider that we each have different 'styles' of communication.

Is your style ideas-driven and one where you like to be the centre of attention?

Is your style one where you need to see the practical side of the subject?

Is your style one where you need to see a logical sequence?

Is your style one where you need to sit back and think for some time before you give a response?

Think of the challenges for each party when you have someone whose communication style is direct and quick interacting with someone who is slow and methodical in their approach?

No one style is 'right' or 'wrong' – they are simply different from each other.

Consider...

❑ Think about a recent time when you disagreed with someone. It doesn't have to be a public disagreement – maybe they don't even *know* you disagreed with them. Just think about your side and their side.

❑ Write down what *you* believe happened.

❑ Now write down what you think *they* believe happened.

❑ Could there possibly be another way of looking at the situation?

❑ How could you have expressed yourself differently to perhaps get a different result?

You Control Your Emotions

Maybe that should read, "You CAN Control Your Emotions" as most people don't. They "react" rather than choose their "response".

"No one can take away my freedom to choose how I will react."
Viktor Frankl

Remember the Eleanor Roosevelt quotation from earlier in the book? If not, here it is again:

"No one can make you feel inferior without your consent."
Eleanor Roosevelt

We can control our emotions. It is up to you if you choose to feel upset, angry, happy or sad. Nothing outside you gives you these emotions – you create them for yourself.

I would encourage you to read Viktor Frankl's book, *'Man's Search for Meaning',* published by Washington Square Press. In it, Frankl describes his time as a Jewish psychiatrist during World War II when he was interned in the Nazi concentration camps.

While many around him gave up during that horrific time, Frankl decided that the captors may be able to imprison his body however they could not imprison his mind. He made a conscious decision to use his skills, knowledge and his power over his emotions and responses to analyse the psychology of the concentration camp – in particular why some people gave up and others did not.

His work lead him to develop a revolutionary approach to psychotherapy known as logotheraphy, or 'man's search for meaning'.

"Happiness does not depend on outward things, but on the way we see them." Leo Tolstoy

---

While some people gave in to what they saw as their fate, Frankl discovered that those who kept going were people who believed they still had 'meaning' in their life – that they had something yet to do.

"Everything can be taken from a man but ...the last of the human freedoms – to choose one's attitude in any given set of circumstances, to choose one's own way." Viktor Frankl

My belief is that if Viktor Frankl was able to control his emotions and his attitude, in such conditions that I pray no one ever experiences again, it is possible for the rest of us in relatively passive circumstances to control ours.

"Nothing can bring you peace but yourself." Ralph Waldo Emerson

Consider...

❑   Write down a situation that regularly sees you getting angry or upset. It could be red traffic lights; it could be a particular person; a particular action...

❑   The next time that event occurs, stop yourself from automatically responding as you have done previously.
❑   Consider the situation.
❑   *Choose* your response.
❑   Act accordingly.
❑   Review the results.

You may decide that being angry or upset *is* the best response. I'm not suggesting that is or isn't the way to go.

What I am suggesting is that by *choosing* your emotional response, you are taking control of your life and, in the words of Viktor Frankl, you are choosing your own way.

False Evidence Appearing Real

"The greatest mistake you can make in life is to be continually fearing you will make one." Elbert Hubbard

FEAR = False Evidence Appearing Real

If you have a chance at discovering and then living your passion and fully realizing your potential, you need to overcome your fears.

"Fear is that little darkroom where negatives are developed." Michael Pritchard

Please note that here we are discussing fear in general as it relates to you achieving your goals, dreams and desires. If you are in a situation where you fear for your personal safety or the safety of your family, please seek immediate assistance. It's one thing to suggest that fear is false evidence appearing real and quite another to acknowledge that there are times when the evidence is true and it is real and you do need to take action.

"Courage is resistance to fear, mastery of fear - not absence of fear." Mark Twain

What is fear?

According to a definition by Princeton University's *Wordnet*, fear is to "be afraid or feel anxious or apprehensive about a possible or probable situation or event".

"Fear is a question: What are you afraid of, and why? Just as the seed of health is in illness, because illness contains information, your fears are a treasure house of self-knowledge if you explore them." Marilyn Ferguson

First, if we analyse that statement, the two words that jump out are "possible" and "probable". Note that nowhere in the definition do they describe a "definite" outcome or event.

So, in other words, fear is imagining what *could* happen, what *might* happen – not what WILL happen! These are possible or probable outcomes – not definite ones.

"The moment we begin to fear the opinions of others and hesitate to tell the truth that is in us, and from motives of policy are silent when we should speak, the divine floods of light and life no longer flow into our souls." Elizabeth Cady Stanton

Fear and Focus

"Fear not that thy life shall come to an end, but rather fear that it shall never have a beginning." John Henry Cardinal Newman

The more you focus upon something the more likely it is to happen. (We will cover this later in the Power of Focus).

If we bring those two elements together you have a situation where, when we allow ourselves to be in a state of "fear" that something bad *could* occur, and then we *focus* on the bad outcome that could occur, not only are we creating additional stress in our lives, we are giving ourselves the best possible chance of *making* that bad thing occur because of how much focus we are placing upon it!

"The truth that many people never understand, until it is too late, is that the more you try to avoid suffering the more you suffer because smaller and more insignificant things begin to torture you in proportion to your fear of being hurt." Thomas Merton

Fear and Stress

"Over the years your bodies become walking autobiographies, telling friends and strangers alike of the minor and major stresses of your lives." Marilyn Ferguson

That brings in the third component we are going to discuss here – stress. Although a certain amount of stress can actually be good for you in particular situations, when you are trying to work through the process of discovering your passion and realizing your full potential, stress is not necessarily the best running mate.

Whenever your body is in a state of acute stress, you often experience symptoms such as the following:

- ❏ Poor memory
- ❏ Confusion
- ❏ Difficulty expressing yourself
- ❏ Increased adrenaline production
- ❏ Increased blood pressure
- ❏ Increased sugar levels

This is because when we are fearful, our body goes into what is known as *fight or flight* mode. In other words, it prepares us to fight the aggressor or run away from the danger.

In order to achieve this, our body increases its heart rate and respiration, pumps extra blood to the muscles and heart (and less blood to parts of the brain), while focusing on how to *physically* remove us from the situation.

That instinct has served us well throughout our evolution to enable us to run from our predators, however when the fear is something intangible from which we cannot run, what happens? Those symptoms stay with us – and in some people who experience stress over a prolonged period of time, they cause other health issues.

"Before you agree to do anything that might add even the smallest amount of stress to your life, ask yourself: What is my truest intention? Give yourself time to let a yes resound within you. When it's right, I guarantee that your entire body will feel it." Oprah Winfrey, O Magazine, October 2002

Fear and Re-Framing

"A woman is like a tea bag- you never know how strong she is until she gets in hot water." Eleanor Roosevelt

One way to deal with fear is to re-frame the situation – or, in other words, look at it from a completely different angle, and in particular remove the extreme emotion and look at the truth and reality of the situation.

"You gain strength, courage and confidence by every experience in which you really stop to look fear in the face. You are able to say to yourself, 'I have lived through this horror. I can take the next thing that comes along.' You must do the thing you think you cannot do." Eleanor Roosevelt

We get so tied up in the emotions, we often lose sight of the facts.

"Nothing in life is to be feared, it is only to be understood. Now is the time to understand more, so that we may fear less." Marie Curie

Consider...

❑   Write about a time when you were fearful.

❑   Describe all the emotions you were feeling.

Consider...

❏   Now, remove the emotions and write down the situation – both the positive and the negative – in a purely factual form. For example, you may have been fearful that you would fail an exam. Discuss the positives and negatives without being emotional – and think about the fact that the more you 'stress' about 'possibly' failing, the more likely you are to fail! * Please note, we are not suggesting that what's happening doesn't have major ramifications – it may well do – but the more you stress about it, the less likely you are to successfully overcome it.

Your Thoughts...

Re-Framing Continued...

Another way to re-frame the situation is to look at the possible outcomes and consider whether you could live with the consequences. Make a decision to choose your response as one of expecting the best possible outcome, not the worst.

If the answer is, "yes, I could live with the possible outcomes (even if they are not pleasant)" and you then say to yourself, "I am only going to focus on the possible *positive* outcomes," you will have gone a long way to reducing the level of fear and stress in your life – and making the way clearer for you to see your passions.

"...when you squelch your toughest judge, that hanging judge at the core of you, there is very little to fear from the ones outside." Sarah, The Duchess of York, Author of "My Story"

This might sound easy – and once you get the hang of it, it is – but it can take some time, especially if you are addicted to being in a state of fear and stress.

"Stress is an ignorant state. It believes that everything is an emergency. Nothing is that important." Natalie Goldberg, O Magazine, October 2002

Consider...

- ❏ Write about a recent situation when you have felt fearful of the possible outcome.

- ❏ Describe that situation.

- ❏ Describe how you felt – what was it about the situation that was leaving you feeling anxious?

Consider...

- ❑ Did the *worst* happen? What *did* happen?

- ❑ Were you able to live with the result?

- ❑ In future, how could you reframe a similar situation to be less fearful and stressed?

You Are An Amazing Individual

"When you have confidence, you can have a lot of fun. And when you have fun, you can do amazing things." Joe Namath

Self-worth is a significant issue for many people.

On the surface you may tell yourself and others that you deserve only the very best that life has to offer, yet deep inside there is a recording playing over and over again telling you that you are not worthy and that there is nothing special about you.

Here is something to consider that fundamentally blows that theory out of the water:

> "Consider the fact that for 3.8 billion years, a period of time older than the Earth's mountains and rivers and oceans, every one of your forebears on both sides has been **attractive** enough to find a mate, **healthy** enough to **reproduce**, and sufficiently blessed by fate and circumstances to live long enough to do so. Not one of your pertinent ancestors was squashed, devoured, drowned, starved, stuck fast, untimely wounded or otherwise deflected from its life's quest of delivering a tiny charge of genetic material to the **right partner** at the **right moment** to perpetuate the only possible sequence of heredity combinations that could result - eventually, astoundingly, and all too briefly - in you."

Excerpt from Bill Bryson's *"A Short History of Nearly Everything"*, 2003, published by Doubleday.

How does believing that you are special help you to discover your passion?

"If you think you can do a thing or think you can't do a thing, you're right." Henry Ford

Without a belief that you are special and unique, it is a challenge to believe that you could possibly have a passion that would be special enough or unique enough that you would want to devote your life to it, let alone spend the time required to discovering it in the first place.

"Have you ever wondered how immigrants, many of whom can't even speak English, come to America and own their own homes and businesses within a short period of time? How do they do it while others – with presumably more advantages – struggle just to make ends meet? What do they know that the rest of us don't?" Marcia A. Steele, Author of "Making it in America"

Consider...

❑ Start with this premise – "You Are Unique!"

❑ Make a list of everything that is unique about *you* - ...and before you say there is nothing unique about you, go back and re-read the quote from Bill Bryson's book. By the very fact that you are here, you are unique. It could be that you have a certain style; a certain way that you do something; some knowledge or skill that you have applied in a different way...

❑ If you have trouble with this activity, consider asking someone close to you to tell you what they believe is special, wonderful and unique about you.

You Deserve The Very Best In Life

Everyone does!

> *"Dignity consists not in possessing honors, but in the consciousness that we deserve them."* *Aristotle*

We all have things that happen in our lives that we think are terrific and other things that we may wish didn't occur, but whatever happens, you deserve the very best that life has to offer. To settle for and believe less is doing an injustice to you and to everyone in your life.

Also, if you believe in God, the Universe or some other 'higher power', are you not doing a disservice to your faith to be less than you can be?

This brings us to an interesting thought:

> *"The minute you settle for less than you deserve, you get even less than you settled for."* *Maureen Dowd, in 'New York Times'*

You don't let yourself want to achieve what you don't think you can have.

> *"Remember that what you believe will depend very much on what you are."* *Noah Porter*

If you truly don't believe that you deserve to have the very best and to be the very best that you can be, you won't let yourself truly want to achieve it in the first place. You may have fleeting thoughts in that general direction but that's all they will be. You won't put your heart and soul into achieving what you don't think you can have.

That's why acknowledging that you deserve the very best is important in being able to discover and live your passion. Without it, while you may work out what you desire, you will never allow yourself to want to achieve it.

"People are always blaming their circumstances for what they are. I don't believe in circumstances. The people who get on in this world are the people who get up and look for the circumstances they want, and, if they can't find them, make them." George Bernard Shaw, "Mrs. Warren's Profession" (1893) act II

Consider...

❑ Consider that you were put on this Earth for a reason and that reason is to be the best you can possibly be.

❑ Write about times in your life when things *have* gone your way.

Consider...

❑ Make a list of terrific major events in your life (it could be events such as your high school graduation; being selected onto a team you really wanted to be on...).

❑ Make a list of terrific *minor* events in your life (it could be as simple as finding a book you have been looking for in a second-hand bookstore).

Who Are You?

"The value of identity of course is that so often with it comes purpose." Richard Grant

- ❑ Who are you?
- ❑ Have you become lost in what you do and in the roles you play – daughter/son, sister/brother, friend?
- ❑ Do you define yourself by your weight, your hair colour, your height?

"If a man happens to find himself, he has a mansion which he can inhabit with dignity all the days of his life." James A. Michener

It is important to recognize that you are not your body, you are not your labels and you are not your roles – you are so much more. Your very essence is so much more.

"The thing that is really hard, and really amazing, is giving up on being perfect and beginning the work of becoming yourself." Anna Quindlen

Former US President, John Quincy Adams summed up this principle when, near the end of his life, he was reportedly asked, "How is John Quincy Adams today?"

"John Quincy Adams is well, thank you, quite well. But the house in which he lives is tottering on its foundations, the windows are shaking, the roof is leaking, the doors are not hanging straight; and I think John Quincy Adams will have to move out of it soon. But John Quincy Adams himself, sir, is quite well, thank you, quite well!"

In his response, Adams made the distinction between the essence of the man and his physical body.

"Self-confidence is the first requisite to great undertakings." Samuel Johnson

69

Consider...

❏ Who are you? List ten 'labels' that are used to describe you. For example daughter, son, student...

1.	
2.	
3.	
4.	
5.	
6.	
7.	
8.	
9.	
10.	

❏ Do you define yourself and/or others by physical appearance? Why?

❏ Do you define yourself and/or others by how much money you/they have? Why?

❏ Do you define yourself and/or others by your/their education and how well you do in school/college? Why?

❏ Are there any other ways you define yourself and/or others? Why?

Consider...

❑ Consider the above questions and your answers. What did you uncover about the way you think of others and yourself?

❑ Now, make a list of 10 of your positive personality characteristics. For example: happy, loving, artistic etc

1.	
2.	
3.	
4.	
5.	
6.	
7.	
8.	
9.	
10.	

Consider...

❑ Think about the differences between the two lists – labels and personality characteristics – and how your use of labels may be holding you back from realizing your potential.

It's Ok To Say, "I'm Good At This!"

"Believe in yourself! Have faith in your abilities! Without a humble but reasonable confidence in your own powers you cannot be successful or happy." Norman Vincent Peale

We live in a society where people who say, "I'm good at this" are thought to be egotistical and arrogant.

We also live in a society where it seems more acceptable to 'beat ourselves up' over our weaknesses than to **'build ourselves up' with our strengths**.

I am going to suggest to you that it is healthy to be able to say that you are good at something!

You don't have to be the best at something to say "I'm good at this!"

Provided you are not trying to put anyone else 'down' in the process, acknowledging your strengths – the things you are good at – is a crucial step to discovering your passion and realizing your potential.

"There is deep wisdom within our very flesh, if we can only come to our senses and feel it." Elizabeth A. Behnke

Consider...

❑   List 20 things you can say, "I'm good at this".

1.	
2.	
3.	
4.	
5.	
6.	
7.	
8.	
9.	
10.	
11.	
12.	
13.	
14.	
15.	
16.	
17.	
18.	
19.	
20.	

Your Thoughts...

Consider...

□ Now, ask your three best friends to list the top 10 things they each believe you are good at – and if you don't feel comfortable asking your friends, then consider asking your teacher, your pastor…

Friend # 1:

1.	
2.	
3.	
4.	
5.	
6.	
7.	
8.	
9.	
10.	

Friend # 2:

1.	
2.	
3.	
4.	
5.	
6.	
7.	
8.	
9.	
10.	

Friend # 3:

1.	
2.	
3.	
4.	
5.	
6.	
7.	
8.	
9.	
10	

Consider...

❑ Review your lists and write down your thoughts on why it is important to be proud of your strengths!

Week 3: The Power of Focus & Self-Talk

"You cannot depend on your eyes when your imagination is out of focus." Mark Twain, A Connecticut Yankee in King Arthur's Court

This week we will explore the power of focus and the power of self-talk. By self-talk I am referring to those thoughts that run though your mind. They can be positive, negative or neutral – and they all have an impact on our ability to realize our potential.

In particular this week we will discuss:

- ❑ Every conscious action is a choice
- ❑ The power of focus
- ❑ What is success?
- ❑ Your perception of yourself
- ❑ What are your excuses?
- ❑ Gratitude

Every Conscious Action Is A Choice

"The best way to predict your future is to create it." Unknown

Everything we do is a choice.

- ❑ You don't have to go to school/college tomorrow.
- ❑ You don't have to smile when someone smiles at you.
- ❑ You don't have to complain when you get a red light.

The consequences of our actions may be positive or negative, but regardless:

Everything we do is a choice.

"The self is not something ready-made, but something in continuous formation through choice of action." John Dewey

❑   Consider your response to the following comment:

"You are exactly in your life where you want to be. By this I mean that you have made choices about what you would do, would not do and how you would react. These choices have lead you to where you are right now. Every conscious action is a choice."

❑   What are your thoughts?

❑   How did you feel reading that statement?

"No one can make you feel inferior without your consent." Eleanor Roosevelt

Yes, it's true that some things happen "to" us. Sometimes we see them as good and sometimes as bad – but either way, we determine our response.

To extract Eleanor Roosevelt's quote a little further;

❑   No one can make you feel inferior,
❑   No one can make you feel angry,
❑   No one can make you feel happy,
❑   No one can make you feel sad…

No one can "make" you feel any emotion.

"Because you are in control of your life. Don't ever forget that. You are what you are because of the conscious and subconscious choices you have made." Barbara Hall, A Summons to New Orleans, 2000

Your Thoughts…

Consider...

- Write about the last time you were angry or sad or upset.

- Why did you allow yourself to feel that way?

- Was your response that someone "made" you feel that particular emotion?

- Now, write about a time recently when you felt really happy.

- Recall what you were doing and why you were happy?

Consider...

- Consider how you feel right at this moment when you are thinking about that happy time. Chances are you feel happy, right?

Nobody is "making" you feel happy – you are doing that to yourself – just as you "make" yourself sad, upset, angry or any other emotional response.

We choose our reactions.

The Power Of Focus

Imagine you are a golfer and between you and the green is a water hazard.

"I'm NOT going to go in the water. I'm NOT going to go in the water," is your mantra as you line up to take your shot.

Where does your ball inevitably go? In the water! Why? Because that's where your "focus" was.

"The key to realizing a dream is to focus not on success but significance - and then even the small steps and little victories along your path will take on greater meaning." Oprah Winfrey, O Magazine, September 2002

Throughout this book, consider where you are placing your focus. Is it on what you want or what you don't want? What tapes do you have playing in your head? Are they telling you that you "can" do something or that you "can't"? Are they wishing for the thing you "want" to happen or hoping that the thing you "don't" want to happen won't (such as the golf shot from above).

"If you want to be truly successful invest in yourself to get the knowledge you need to find your unique factor. When you find it and focus on it and persevere your success will blossom." Sidney Madwed

---

Consider...

❑ Write about something that is an issue for you. For example, it might be your grades.

❑ Consider the following: Is your focus on what you don't want? For example, if your issue is your grades, is your focus on possibly failing?

❑ If so, what are you attracting more of into your life?

Consider...

Remember the golf example – where you place your focus is what you attract.

❑ How can you change your focus?

What Is Success?

Many people believe that if only they can discover their passion, they will be "successful" – but what *is* success to you?

- ❑   For some people it's having a million dollars.
- ❑   For other people it's having a happy and loving family.
- ❑   For others it's being able to take long holidays several times a year.
- ❑   For you it might be all or none of the above.

I am going to suggest to you that success is really a *feeling* more than it is an acquisition of any thing or things.

Consider...

- ❑   Write about what it would mean for you to be "successful".

- ❑   What are you doing?

- ❑   What do you have?

Consider...

❑ What are you giving?

❑ How do you *feel*?

"Many of life's failures are people who did not realize how close they were to success when they gave up." Thomas A. Edison

Your Thoughts...

Your Perception of Yourself

"No man has the right to dictate what other men should perceive, create or produce, but all should be encouraged to reveal themselves, their perceptions and emotions, and to build confidence in the creative spirit." Ansel Adams

In Week 2 we asked the question "Who Are You" particularly in relation to the labels you may use in describing yourself and others.

This week we will focus on your perception of yourself in the following areas:

- ❑ Physically
- ❑ Emotionally
- ❑ Financially
- ❑ Spiritually

"If the doors of perception were cleansed everything would appear to man as it is, infinite. For man has closed himself up, till he sees all things thru' chinks of his cavern." William Blake

Consider...

Taking each area at a time, complete the following tables, noting what you believe to be positive about yourself and negative about yourself.

For example, physically, you may put that you have "great hair" in the Positive column and in the Negative column you may put that you don't like the fact that you have seven toes on one foot.

Whatever you write, do not judge yourself. Just be honest. We will review your responses.

My Perception of me: **Physically**

POSITIVE	NEGATIVE

Your Thoughts…

My Perception of me: **Emotionally**

POSITIVE	NEGATIVE

Your Thoughts…

My Perception of me: **Financially**

POSITIVE	NEGATIVE

Your Thoughts…

My Perception of me: **Spiritually**

POSITIVE	NEGATIVE

Your Thoughts...

Consider...

- ❏ Look at the Negative columns for each characteristic.
- ❏ When you talk about those characteristics, have you used any emotive words such as "I hate"? Or if you were talking about those characteristics, would you use such words as "hate"? Why?

- ❏ If so, consider the self-talk you are giving yourself.

- ❏ Take each negative in turn and write down any labels you have given yourself – or you have allowed others to give you – such as "fat", "stupid", "worthless".

Consider...

Now, we are going to re-frame each of those labels away from emotional labels to purely factual terms. (You may wish to refer back to the chapter on Fear and Re-Framing).

- ❏ Take each label in turn and write it in factual terms (eg instead of "fat" it might be "10lb over my ideal weight")

Once you have a starting point that is emotion-neutral you are in a better place to do something about it.

We will cover goal setting and achieving a little later...

What Are Your Excuses?

"All men should strive to learn before they die what they are running from, and to, and why." James Thurber

We all have an arsenal of excuses for why we are not living up to our full potential.

"You have to value doing what is right along with what is easy"
Suze Orman, Author of "The Courage to be Rich"

Your excuses could also simply be that you are looking at the **problem** instead of the **opportunity**.

Consider this quote:

"You may have read the proverbial story of two shoe salesmen sent to Africa 50 years ago. One reported to his office, "All the natives here walk about barefoot and so there is no market," whereas the other reported, "All the natives here walk about barefoot, so there is a tremendous opportunity to sell shoes." Given the same circumstances, one person sees a problem, the other an opportunity." Simon Tupman, Author of "Why Entrepreneurs Should Eat Bananas"

Consider...

❑ Make a list of 10 things you have wanted to do in your life but have never done.

1.	
2.	
3.	
4.	
5.	
6.	
7.	
8.	
9.	
10.	

❏ Now, be totally honest with yourself and discover the 'excuses' you have been giving yourself for not having achieved those things.

Think back to the Motivation chapter. It would have been easy to have used breaking your arm as an 'excuse' for not having been able to claim your prize-money. Instead you rose to the challenge and achieved your objective.

❏ Go back to your list and write out what you 'might have been able to do' to rise to the challenge.

Your Thoughts...

Gratitude

"If you have no friends to share or rejoice in your success in life - if you cannot look back to those whom you owe gratitude, or forward to those to whom you ought to afford protection, still it is no less incumbent on you to move steadily in the path of duty; for your active excretions are due not only to society; but in humble gratitude to the Being who made you a member of it." Walter Scott

You may wonder what gratitude has to do with discovering your passion and realizing your potential?

"Gratitude is the memory of the heart." Italian Proverb

Being grateful for what you have is one of the foundation blocks for being able to attract into your life what you want. It also produces a state in your body that is conducive to working out what that is!

"Feeling gratitude and not expressing it is like wrapping a present and not giving it." William Arthur Ward

You can download your free Gratitude Journal at www.LeighStJohn.com.

Consider...

❏ Write about something or someone for which you are truly grateful.

❏ How do you 'feel' about that person or event. That's the feeling we want to tap into.

❏ Consider starting a "Gratitude Journal" and every morning and evening writing five to ten things that happened that day about which you are grateful.

You can download a free Gratitude Journal from www.LeighStJohn.com.

Your Thoughts...

Week 4: Self-Sabotage

This week we will look at two basic areas of self-sabotage:
- ❑ Stop blaming
- ❑ Fear of success
- ❑ Learned helplessness
- ❑ Victim or Survivor?

"It seems to me that people have vast potential. Most people can do extraordinary things if they have the confidence or take the risks. Yet most people don't. They sit in front of the telly and treat life as if it goes on forever." Philip Adams

---

Stop Blaming

"It is no use to blame the looking glass if your face is awry."
Nikolai Gogol

Remember this from an earlier chapter?

"You are exactly in your life where you want to be. By this I mean that you have made choices about what you would do, would not do and how you would react. These choices have lead you to where you are right now. Every conscious action is a choice."

Are you blaming others for your situation?

"The best years of your life are the ones in which you decide your problems are your own. You don't blame them on your mother, the ecology, or the President. You realize that you control your own destiny." *Albert Ellis*

Consider...

❑ Write about something you wanted to do in your life and believe someone else 'stopped' you from achieving that objective.

❑ Write out what you wanted.

❑ Write out what they 'did'.

Consider...

❑   Write out what you could have done differently (think back to the motivation chapter).

❑   Why have you allowed yourself to blame someone else for the situation for all this time?

❑   How could you reframe your memory of what happened so that you take ownership of your part in the situation?

Fear of Success

"Procrastination is the fear of success." Denis Waitley

Fear of success stops many people from achieving their goals and realizing their full potential.

Fear of success comes in a variety of forms:

- ❑ Fear that you will get what you want and you still won't be happy
- ❑ Fear that it will all disappear at any moment and so you tell yourself "there's less distance to fall if I just stay down here with other 'unsuccessful' people"
- ❑ Fear that people won't like you
- ❑ Fear that 'success' is the end of the journey – then what?

"Always bear in mind that your own resolution to succeed is more important than any one thing." Abraham Lincoln

Consider...

Consider answering the following questions about your life in general or about any specific situations that may come to mind.

- ❑ Why don't I believe I can be successful?

- ❑ Who am I afraid of hurting or intimidating if I am successful?

- ❑ Who do I believe won't like me if I am successful?

- ❑ Once I achieve 'success' what do I intend to do next?

- ❑ How motivated am I to be successful?

Consider...

Now consider the following:

- ❑ In what ways do I sabotage my own success?

- ❑ What is the worst thing that could happen if people don't like me because I am successful?

- ❑ How could I do my best to ensure that I don't hurt or intimidate people?

- ❑ What could I do to increase my motivation to be successful – and my belief that I really can do it?

Consider...

One final consideration – you are ALREADY successful in many areas.

- ❑ Make a list of everything you can think of during your life where you have been successful.

- ❑ What did that success feel like?

- ❑ Was it a good or bad feeling?

- ❑ What can you learn from that feeling?

Learned Helplessness

While researching links between fear and learning, Martin Seligman and his colleagues uncovered a behavior pattern that resulted in the discovery of an interesting phenomenon.

The first part of this scenario is that when dogs were placed in a situation from which there was no escape and were subjected to a negative impulse, they learned to put up with the impulse and wait for it to subside. They would try to escape for some time and in the end they would give up. They knew there was no alternative.

The second and startling part of this scenario is that when the same dogs were then *not* confined – that is, they were able to remove themselves from the negative impulse – they remained where they were, put up with the impulse and waited for it to subside. They had come to *believe* there was no alternative.

They had learned to be helpless!

This phenomenon is not only the domain of our fluffy companions – humans exhibit the same behavior. When they believed that whatever they did was futile, they gave up and experienced a lack of motivation to explore alternatives.

Your Thoughts...

Consider...

- Write about a situation where you have been trying and trying and trying yet you have not been able to be successful.

- Have you given up? Why?

- What might have happened if you kept trying and perhaps explored a different approach?

- What did you have to tell yourself to get yourself to believe it was futile to keep trying?

Consider...

Interestingly, Seligman also discovered that our "explanatory style", or what we tell ourselves as the reasons for our setbacks, is in direct correlation to our ability to persevere and is also linked to the health of our immune system.

- What do you tell yourself when you have setbacks?

Victim Or Survivor

Which are you?

When we believe something happens *to* us, we sometimes take on the role of 'victim' (refer to the previous examples of learned helplessness).

"Everybody has difficult years, but a lot of times the difficult years end up being the greatest years of your whole entire life." Brittany Murphy

Whether you see yourself as a victim or as a survivor, the event will still be the same, however your *reaction* will be different – and remember, we can choose our reactions.

"There is only one optimist. He has been here since man has been on this earth, and that is "man" himself. If we hadn't had such a magnificent optimism to carry us through all these things, we wouldn't be here. We have survived it on our optimism." Edward Steichen

Consider...

❑   Think about something in your life that has happened that has left a scar or hurt and pain.

❑   How has that hurt and pain made you a better person?

❑   How has that hurt and pain made you more understanding or tolerant?

❑   How have you been able to use what you have learned through experiencing that situation to help others? – and if you haven't, how could you?

Week 5: Your Authentic Self

"If a man is called to be a street sweeper, he should sweep streets even as Michelangelo painted, or Beethoven played music, or Shakespeare wrote poetry. He should sweep streets so well that all the hosts of heaven and earth will pause to say, here lived a great street sweeper who did his job well." Martin Luther King Jr.

We have explored the labels people use in describing themselves and various roles they play.

In this chapter, we are going to delve a little further into your *authentic* self.

So, what is your authentic self?

It's the core of who you are. It is a combination of your values, your gifts, and your personality – and is guided by your own moral compass.

If you are to discover your passion, you need to understand and appreciate your authentic self.

Values Inventory

What are your values? For example, do you value hard work? (and it's ok to say, "no" if that doesn't apply to you! You need to be honest).
- ❑ Consider the following list of values and circle or tick any that apply to you.
- ❑ Add any values you have that are not on the list.

❑ Integrity	❑ Communication
❑ Honesty	❑ Fairness
❑ Compassion	❑ Family
❑ Respect	❑ Strength
❑ Continuous Improvement	❑ Freedom
❑ Humility	❑ Tolerance
❑ Practicality	❑ Quality
❑ Harmony	❑ Efficiency
❑ Perseverance	❑ Gratitude
❑ Growth	❑ Achievement
❑ Development	❑ Commitment
❑ Stability	❑ Refinement
❑ Elegance	❑ Relationships
❑ Contribution	❑ Power

When it comes time to work out your passion(s), remember your passion(s) must align to your values.

Your Thoughts...

106

Gifts Inventory

Consider...

What are your gifts? For example, are you a natural teacher?

- ❑ Consider the following list of gifts and circle or tick any that apply to you.
- ❑ Add any gifts you have that are not on the list.

❑	Teaching	❑	Building things
❑	Music	❑	Fixing things
❑	Art	❑	Creativity
❑	Writing	❑	Healing
❑	Technology	❑	Inspiring
❑	Communicating	❑	Leading
❑	Mathematics	❑	Organizing
❑	Working with Animals	❑	Researching
❑	Sports	❑	Logic

When it comes time to work out your passion(s), remember your passion(s) will be in the areas of your gifts.

Your Thoughts...

Personality Inventory

What is your authentic personality? For example, are you naturally a loving person even if in your present situation you believe you are not able to express those feelings?

- ❑ Consider the following list of gifts and circle or tick any that apply to you.
- ❑ Add any gifts you have that are not on the list.
- ❑ Note, some of these personality traits may also be considered 'values'.

A group of two hundred executives were asked what makes a person successful. Eighty per cent listed enthusiasm as the most important quality." Author Unknown

---

- ❑ Warm
- ❑ Analytical
- ❑ Competitive
- ❑ Loyal
- ❑ Self-reliant
- ❑ Caring
- ❑ Dedicated
- ❑ Loving
- ❑ Refined
- ❑ Stable
- ❑ Introspective
- ❑ Dominant
- ❑ Affable
- ❑ Problem-solving

- ❑ Enthusiastic
- ❑ Inquisitive
- ❑ Reflective
- ❑ Elegant
- ❑ Practical
- ❑ Careful
- ❑ Courteous
- ❑ Intuitive
- ❑ Self-controlled
- ❑ Perfectionist
- ❑ Welcoming
- ❑ Critical
- ❑ Judgmental
- ❑ Friendly

When it comes time to work out your passion(s), remember your passion(s) will be ones that allow you to make full and open use of your authentic personality.

Week 6: The Power of Energy

"Every time you don't follow your inner guidance, you feel a loss of energy, loss of power, a sense of spiritual deadness." Shakti Gawain

You feel positive and negative energy all the time and are only occasionally conscious of it.

Think of walking into a room when you can "feel the tension". This is energy.

Think of how you feel when a beaming smile from the other side of the room suddenly catches your eye. This is energy.

The positive and negative energy we allow into our life and our environment is controllable to a certain extent – and our *reaction* to it is definitely controllable.

Everything Has Energy

If you consider that everything around you has energy, with what type of energy are you surrounding yourself?

Consider...

Consider that you have a 'mute' button where negative energy is concerned. You can choose not to allow it to affect you or to remove yourself from the situation entirely.

❑   Make a list of the ten people with whom you spend most of your time.
❑   What is the energy of each of those relationships?

Person	Energy

Consider...

- If the energy in any relationship is other than positive, what can you do to change it or remove yourself from the situation?

Think about your friends at school/college.
- What is the energy there?
- If the energy is other than positive, what can you do to change it or remove yourself from that particular group?

Think about the movies you watch, the books you read.
- What energy do they have?
- Is that energy supporting you?

Think about the food you eat.
- Is it highly processed or natural?
- Is the energy in the food you are consuming supporting you?

Think about the words you use, the things you say.
- Is the energy you are expressing supporting you?

The Energy of Thoughts

"...happiness gives us the energy which is the basis of health."
Henri-Frédéric Amiel

Have you ever considered the energy of your thoughts?

Why is it that positive thoughts produce one set of effects within us, negative thoughts produce another and the Zen approach (not seeing anything as good or bad) produces yet another?

"Energy is the essence of life. Every day you decide how you're going to use it by knowing what you want and what it takes to reach that goal, and by maintaining focus." Oprah Winfrey

Modern medicine is slowly accepting the reality of "mind over matter" in that we can control our physical bodies by the thoughts that we think – and just how much control we truly have is a subject that attracts a great deal of debate.

"I merely took the energy it takes to pout and wrote some blues."
Duke Ellington

Consider...

❑   What are your thoughts about whether you will be able to discover your passion and realize your full potential?

❑   What thoughts do you have about who you are?

❑   Are your thoughts serving you and advancing you?

Reflection Time...

□ At this point, go back through your notes and read what you have written.

□ What ideas or challenges for you have been the most important so far?

□ List the three things you have learned or further explored that you believe will be most crucial to you discovering your passion and realizing your potential.

1.	
2.	
3.	

□ Make a list of five successes you have had since starting this journey.

1.	
2.	
3.	
4.	
5.	

Your Thoughts...

Part 2: Embracing the Power

CONGRATULATIONS!!!

You have made it through the tough section – the part where you begin to understand the power of just how special you really are, and begin to gain an insight into three basic questions –

1. Who you are
2. Where you are and
3. Why you are there

From here, we will examine issues such as:

- ❑ What do you love?
- ❑ Discovering Your Passion.
- ❑ Role Models.
- ❑ Developing Certainty.
- ❑ The Secret to Getting What You Want.
- ❑ Taking the First Steps.

"The greatest danger for most of us is not that we aim too high and we miss it, but we aim too low and reach it." Michelangelo

Consider...

In the remainder of your journey through discovering your passion, it is important to have a Cheer Squad of people who are on your side.

❑ List the names of at least three and as many as five people who you believe would actively encourage and support you during this journey.

❑ Why have you chosen those particular people?

❑ If you haven't already told them about this process, tell them now and ask them whether they would volunteer to be a member of your Cheer Squad.

Consider...

❑ Let them know that their role is to congratulate you, to encourage you, to support you and generally to cheer you along your journey.

❑ While it is fine for them to challenge you, their role is *not* to continually tell you why it won't work – you will have plenty of other people who will willingly take on that role without even being asked!

Week 7: What Do You Love?

"There is no pay check that can equal the feeling of contentment that comes from being the person you are meant to be." Oprah Winfrey

Now that you have cleared the clutter and adjusted your focus, the next step in discovering your passion and realizing your potential is to analyze what you love to do because that will be at the core of your passion.

When people are asked, "what do you love?" they give a variety of responses including:

- ❑ Providing specific examples
- ❑ "I have no idea"
- ❑ "So many things I can't name just a few"
- ❑ "I don't love anything"

We will take all of those responses and more into consideration in the following exercise.

Consider...

Write down your responses to the following and where appropriate list as many responses as you can.

If you find that you have difficulty in coming up with an answer, persevere a little longer and then if no answer comes, move on to the next question. Once you are done, revisit any questions you had difficulty in answering.

❑ What do you love to do? Why?

❑ What do you NOT like doing? Why?

❑ When you were a small child, what did you want to be when you grew up? Why? What was it about being or doing that type of job that appealed to you?

Consider...

❑　If you had a free day where you could be doing anything at all, where would you be and what would you be doing? Why?

❑　Do you have a dream you have never shared with anyone? Why would you like to achieve that dream?

❑　What makes you smile? Why?

❑　If you have a general idea of what your passion is eg travel – what is it about travel that you love?

Consider...

- ❏ What would you be doing for a job even if they didn't pay you for it? Why?

- ❏ Are you a leader or a follower? Both are great – which do you prefer? Why?

- ❏ What are your top three memorable moments from your life to date? Why?

- ❏ What are your top three favorite characteristics that you see in yourself? Why?

Consider...

❑ What is your favorite section in a bookstore? Why?

❑ What is your favorite section in a newspaper? Why?

❑ What would you do if you knew you couldn't fail? Why?

❑ Do you prefer indoor or outdoor activities? Why?

❑ Do you like to be the centre of attention or part of the crowd? Why?

❑ If you found out you only had days to live, in addition to not having spent more time with loved ones, what would you regret not having done in your life? Why?

Week 8: Discovering Your Passion

People often say that this or that person has not yet found himself. But the self is not something one finds, it is something one creates. Thomas Szasz, "Personal Conduct," The Second Sin, 1973

This is where most people stumble and get stuck.

After having completed the last exercise, they either have no idea what their passion is or they scream that they have too many.

We will look at the following, in particular, in this chapter:

- ❏ Too Many Passions?
- ❏ What if I am on the Wrong Track?
- ❏ Pulling It All Together

Stay with the process and we will work through how you can focus on the underlying – and true – passion in your responses.

"You must give some time to your fellow men. Even if it's a little thing, do something for others -- something for which you get no pay but the privilege of doing it." Albert Schweitzer

---

Additional Questions

"You have to leave the city of your comfort and go into the wilderness of your intuition. What you'll discover will be wonderful. What you'll discover is yourself." Alan Alda

Consider...

Write down your responses to the following:

- ❏ In what areas are you really talented – better than most?

- ❏ What have you achieved/accomplished/proud of?

Consider...

- ❑ Do you envy anyone? Why?

- ❑ Whose life would you like to have? Why?

- ❑ Leaving aside whether you agree with cloning, what if you were presented with a baby clone of *you* – what would you encourage him/her to pursue?

- ❑ Who do you admire? Why?

Consider...

- ❑ What would you do to make the world a better place for you, your friends and family, and for others?

- ❑ What do you want your passion to give to you?

- ❑ Ask your three most trusted friends to answer the following questions:
    - o What do you think I am good at?
    - o What do you think are my top 5 natural talents?
    - o What do you think my passion could be?
    - o How am I getting in my own way and self-sabotaging?

Consider...

❑ How do you want to be remembered? Not how you 'think' you will
   be remembered, but how you would design the epitaph of your life –
   your ideal life?

Your Thoughts...

Too Many Passions?

"Choose a job you love, and you will never have to work a day in your life."   Confucius

It is not uncommon to reach this point and feel that you have too many passions and you could not possibly follow all of them!

You will be reassured to know that while it may seem there are too many, chances are there is a way to form them into a single unit – or at most two where one is for a career and the other is for a hobby or pastime.

We will be working on that process in "Pulling It All Together".

Your Thoughts...

Pulling It All Together

"Use what talent you possess: the woods would be very silent if no birds sang except those that sang best." Henry Van Dyke

You have put in so much work to get to this point: **CONGRATULATIONS!**

"Do not follow where the path may lead. Go instead where there is no path and leave a trail." Harold R. McAlindon

Now we are going to review your responses and pull them together to discover what your passion really is.

"Whatever you can do or dream you can, begin it. Boldness has genius, power, and magic in it. Begin it now." Goethe

Step 1 – Review The Pieces...

- ❏ Review your responses to "What Do You Love".
- ❏ What words are repeated in your responses? List as many as you can find.

- ❏ What themes do you find that keep cropping up? List as many as you can find.

- ❏ Review your responses to "Additional Questions".
- ❏ What words are repeated in your responses? List as many as you can find.

- ❏ What themes do you find that keep cropping? List as many as you can find.

Consider...

❏ When you talked about anyone you envied or admired, what was it about them that you envied or admired?

❏ What was your response to the question about what you would do if you knew you couldn't fail?

❏ Which of these words most describes you?
   - Practical
   - Outrageous
   - Thinker
   - Planner

❏ Explore your inventories from Week 5. Chose your strongest three characteristics from each inventory.

1.	
2.	
3.	

Consider...

❏ What are the five elements your passion must have for you to feel fulfilled? For example, it could be "travel, personal growth, meeting people, writing and international cuisine".

1.	
2.	
3.	
4.	
5.	

Hint

Do you see where this is going? For example, if you take the last example, that person's passion could be:

- o   Travel Writer
- o   International Food Critic
- o   Teaching in the areas of Travel, Food etc.
- o   International Tour Guide
- o   …and so on.

Your Thoughts…

Step 2 – It's Not About You...

Consider the following statement:

Your passion will not be about *you* – it will ultimately be about serving others in some way.

❏   What insights does that statement give you?

❏   For example, if you take the "Hint" from above, while that person's passion could be any one of those things, ultimately, it's about giving rather than receiving.

"It is one of the most beautiful compensations of this life that no man can sincerely try to help another without helping himself." Ralph Waldo Emerson

Your Thoughts...

Step 3 – Think Outside The Square...

It was once a ridiculous notion to consider buying water in bottles and now it is commonplace.

❑ When you put the pieces of your puzzle together, don't just look for the traditional. Think outside the square.

❑ What other opportunities could be right before you?

❑ If you had to come up with three possible passions based on combining the most important elements of all the above exercises, what might they be?

1.	
2.	
3.	

❑ Do any of these resonate with you? Why? How?

Step 4 – Remove Limitations...

"Keep away from people who try to belittle your ambitions. Small people always do that, but the really great make you feel that you, too, can become great." Mark Twain

So, imagine yourself a few years down the track. You have discovered your passion is to travel the world as a writer. Great!

You just remembered you are a single mother with two young children. Not so great? Wrong!!!

I once worked with a woman who went through this exact process and who came up with exactly that passion and had exactly those limitations. What she decided to do was travel the world with her children writing for various publications.

She did her homework, gained further training and secured paid positions with two publications and was a 'stringer' (a writer who submits to various publications) to several others. She sold up everything she had and together with her children commenced the journey of a lifetime.

While this may not be the journey for you, I mention it to illustrate that it is possible.

Remove any limitations you may have about what you can or cannot do – remember, the four-minute mile was once impossible, too.

Step 5 – Any Desire Is Ok...

"I only hope that we never lose sight of one thing - that it was all started by a mouse." Walt Disney

Acknowledge to yourself that any desire, any passion is ok – it doesn't have to be the traditional success markers such as something that will provide wealth.

Your passion may be to be a great sportsperson.

"Go confidently in the direction of your dreams. Live the life you have imagined." Henry David Thoreau

Step 6 – Focus On The Emotions...

When discovering your passion, remember to focus on the emotions, not the job.

For example, you may think your passion is to be a teacher.

Rather than focus on teaching at this stage of discovery, focus on what it *is* about teaching that you love or believe you would love. This way you are not limiting yourself to just the role of teacher. You may in fact find that there is another passion hidden within.

"I could never convince the financiers that Disneyland was feasible because dreams offer too little collateral." Walt Disney

Step 7 – Search For The Core...

"It's never too late to be what you might have been."   George
Elliot

You may think that your passion is not just one thing.

Think about Oprah Winfrey. She has a range of interests however her underlying passion is to help people to be the best they can be.

From that point – from the point of her core passion – she is able to pursue a range of interests that support that passion.

"Be patient toward all that is unsolved in your heart and try to love the questions themselves like locked rooms and like books that are written in a very foreign tongue. Do not now seek the answers, which cannot be given you because you would not be able to live them. And the point is, to live everything. Live the questions now. Perhaps you will find them gradually, without noticing it, and live along some distant day into the answer."
Rainer Maria Rilke, Letters to a Young Poet

Consider

- ❑ Look back through the exercises in this book. What are some of the main themes that keep coming up over and over again?

What Is Your Purpose?

"The happiness of a man in this life does not consist in the absence but in the mastery of his passions." Alfred Lord Tennyson

So, now comes crunch-time.

What is your purpose – your core passion?

"My passions were all gathered together like fingers that made a fist. Drive is considered aggression today; I knew it then as purpose." Bette Davis

Consider...

❏ Have you worked out what it is that you want to achieve in life?

❏ How might you go about it?

If you have still not at least come close to discovering your passion, consider working with a trusted friend and have them challenge you with regard to the questions covered in Weeks 7 and 8.

You DO know what your passion is – you might just be having trouble *seeing* it.

Your Thoughts...

What If I'm On the Wrong Track?

> *"Driving down the wrong road and knowing it,*
> *The fork years behind, how many have thought*
> *To pull up on the shoulder and leave the car*
> *Empty, strike out across the fields; and how many*
> *Are still mazed among dock and thistle,*
> *Seeking the road they should have taken?"*
> Damon Knight, The Man in the Tree

OK, so you have worked out what your passion is and you realize you have been climbing a ladder that's been up against the wrong wall?

Move the ladder! It's that simple.

Note, I said "simple", not necessarily "easy".

Consider...

❑ Have I been going down the wrong track?

❑ What can I do to change my direction?

Declaring Your Purpose

By now you will have discovered your purpose – or at least be much closer to knowing what it is.

It's now time to start 'wearing' it publicly.

Consider...

- ❑ Rally your Cheer Squad together and tell them you have an important announcement to make. Even if you are not 100% certain that you have discovered your passion, still complete this activity.
- ❑ Tell them that this is going to be a celebration and arrange for someone to bring the sodas, someone to bring the food etc – just as you would for a party.
- ❑ Once your Cheer Squad is gathered around, declare your passion – or what you have come up with so far – to them and thank them for their role in the process.
- ❑ Let them know that this is just one step of many and you are now about to continue the journey to realizing your full potential.
- ❑ Ask them for their feedback and encouragement.

Your Thoughts...

Week 9: Inspiration From Others

What's that saying, "No man is an island"?

On the road to living your passion and realizing your potential, you may want to turn to and tap into others for inspiration.

In this chapter, we will examine:

- ❑ Role Models
- ❑ MasterMind Groups
- ❑ You As The Role Model

"Man stands in his own shadow and wonders why it's dark." Zen Proverb

Role Models

"I think of a hero as someone who understands the degree of responsibility that comes with his freedom." Bob Dylan

Chose your role models wisely and they can provide a wealth of information and inspiration.

Role models are not people you want to be like exactly. Rather they are people whose talents, qualities, abilities or other attributes you would like to model and adapt into your own life.

Role modelling is an important step in realizing your full potential as it provides us with practical examples of people who are overcoming the obstacles and making it happen. This in turn inspires us and helps us to recognize that we, too, can move past setbacks and achieve our goals.

"What sunshine is to flowers, smiles are to humanity." George Eliot

Consider...

❑ Think about your passion – or at least the areas you have come up with so far.

❑ List three people who are currently working successfully in that field who you would like to use as role models.

1.	
2.	
3.	

Consider...

- ❏ Do some research on each to find out:
    - ○ How did they start?

    - ○ What hurdles they faced?

    - ○ Did they need any specific training?

    - ○ What mistakes have they made?

    - ○ How has their determination paid off?

    - ○ What have they achieved?

    - ○ What do they still want to achieve?

- ❏ What is it about each of them that inspires you?

- ❏ How can you use this information to help you realize your potential?

- ❏ Are there any role models that you could interview in person?

MasterMind Groups

The concept of the MasterMind Group was introduced by Napoleon Hill in his well-known work, "Think And Grow Rich".

He defined the MasterMind principle as follows:

"The coordination of knowledge and effort of two or more people, who work toward a definite purpose, in the spirit of harmony."

"No two minds ever come together without thereby creating a third, invisible intangible force, which may be likened to a third mind." Napoleon Hill

Essentially, it is a group of people who meet regularly to explore a particular topic or topics.

You brainstorm ideas, provide feedback and support to each other.

"We allow our ignorance to prevail upon us and make us think we can survive alone, alone in patches, alone in groups, alone in races, even alone in genders." Maya Angelou

Your Thoughts...

Consider...

Consider setting up your own MasterMind Group.

❏   What do you want it to achieve?

❏   What topics do you want it to explore?

❏   Who would you like to invite?

❏   How often would you like to meet?

❏   Where and when would you like to meet?

❏   What support would you like it to provide?

You As The Role Model

"We make a living by what we get. We make a life by what we give." -- Winston Churchill

This may be a new idea for some people, however consider how you might be able to be a role model to others.

Just the knowledge that someone looks to you to provide inspiration and guidance can sometimes be enough to help us to lift our game and push that little bit harder to achieve our goals.

"The best way to find yourself is to lose yourself in the service of others." Mahatma Gandhi

Consider...

You may be relatively young, but you can be a role model to someone even younger.

❑ Is there anyone who has ever told you they admire you?

❑ What did they say?

❑ How did you feel?

❑ Are there any local groups or churches where you could volunteer your services as a mentor or coach?

Week 10: Developing Certainty

"Intention includes Hope, which includes expectation."
Christopher Westra - I Create Reality

"I believe that uncertainty is really my spirit's way of whispering, 'I'm in flux. I can't decide for you. Something is off-balance here.'" Oprah Winfrey

What would you do if you had CERTAINTY that you would succeed?

Regardless of your spiritual beliefs, the power of faith has seen people overcome incredible hurdles and achieve amazing feats.

Consider this statement:

"Casual wishes and desires are not pursued primarily because we do not believe."

"Whenever you are asked if you can do a job, tell 'em, 'Certainly I can!' Then get busy and find out how to do it." Theodore Roosevelt

Certainty of Passion...

❑   Think about your passion – or the general ideas you have about what your passion could be.

❑   On a scale of 1 to 100, where is your level of excitement about that passion?

| 1 | | 100 |

❑   If it is not up around the 100 mark, why isn't it?

❑   Do you need to revisit your ideas or possibly simply allow yourself to get excited?

Consider...

❑ On a scale of 1 to 100, where is your level of certainty that you can achieve your goal?

| 1 | | 100 |

❑ If it is not up around the 100 mark, why isn't it?

❑ What can you do to increase your level of certainty?

Live As Though It Already Exists...

❑ What could you change in your world to begin going through your days as though you are already living your passion?

❑ What actions could you take to reinforce to yourself that you are moving toward living your passion and realizing your full potential?

Week 11: The Secret To Getting What You Want

In this chapter we will examine why so many traditional goal setting processes do not work and explore the secret to getting what you want out of life.

In particular we will look at:

- ❑ Your Habits
- ❑ Realizing You Have the Power
- ❑ Do it "until"…

Habits

Habits are things we have done over and over and over again to the point where we don't need to 'think' about them.

Think about this...

Why is it that people who are so intoxicated they can barely put a sentence together, are sometimes still capable of getting behind the wheel of a car and driving home?

It's because they have developed the HABIT of driving. In order to simply go through the motions of driving the car, they require little if anything from their higher brain functions.

Why is it that these same intoxicated people, when driving home, are far more likely to kill themselves or others?

While they may be able to perform the habit of driving, should anything that requires a higher brain function (such the quick reasoning skills necessary if someone unexpectedly pulls out in front of them) their brain is too chemically impaired to successfully navigate the problem and disaster can be the result.

Some habits can be useful – some habits can be detrimental.

Now, consider how difficult you are making it for yourself if you have a range of well-established HABITS (reactions, patterns – call them what you like) where you simply REACT without thinking - and, instead of creating *new* habits as part of your plan, you are simply making lists of what you want to achieve and how you expect to go about it!

Do you have the habit of coming home and immediately sitting in front of the television?

Do you have the habit of sleeping in so long that you are always running late?

Consider...

❑   What habits have you developed that are holding you back (it could even be something that you say to yourself over and over again that is not serving you).

❑   What NEW habits could you develop that would help you to grow and to realize your potential?

"We are what we repeatedly do. Excellence, therefore, is not an act but a habit." Aristotle

Your Thoughts...

Realizing You Have the Power

"Believe that problems do have answers, that they can be overcome, and that you can solve them." Norman Vincent Peale

There are those – myself included – who believe we only have desires and passions that we have the capability of achieving.

To put that another way, I have no desire to become a world famous baseball player – which is probably a good thing as the safest place to be when I am throwing or batting is where I am aiming! I have no natural talent for any sports involving throwing or batting.

I do, however, have a range of other natural talents – and they are in line with my passions and my purpose.

"Finally, when I was at my lowest ebb emotionally, physically, and financially, I learned about the power of thought as an instrument for success or failure. I came to realize that failure is basically the result of failure thinking. I learned that the right use of my mind could become the key to healthy, happy, prosperous, successful living. As soon as I grasped this wonderful success secret, the tide began to change!" Catherine Ponder, Author of *"The Dynamic Laws of Prosperity*

Consider...

❑ Think about your purpose.
❑ List your abilities and all the elements that are working in your favor to live your passion and achieve your potential.

Do it "Until"...

"How long should you try? Until." Jim Rohn

Will you discover your passion and realize your potential immediately? Maybe you will!

What if you don't?

How long will you keep pressing on?

Consider a baby learning to walk – do we give up on them the first, second or third time they try to take a step and fall?

How long you continue to persevere is up to you.

Your Thoughts...

152

Reflection Time

It's time to look at the journey you have taken thus far and reward yourself for your progress.

"We need to prepare ourselves for he possibility that sometimes big changes follow from small events, and that sometimes these changes can happen very quickly." Malcolm Gladwell, Author of "The Tipping Point"

Consider...

- ❑ What are the most important insights you have had so far?

- ❑ What changes are you already noticing in your life?

- ❑ How much time are you spending on realizing your potential and living your passion?

"There is no happiness except in the realization that we have accomplished something." Henry Ford

---

Week 12: Developing Your Goal Process

"Most of the important things in the world have been accomplished by people who have kept on trying when there seemed to be no hope at all." Dale Carnegie

> *"In the absence of clearly-defined goals, we become strangely loyal to performing daily trivia until ultimately we become enslaved by it."* Robert Heinlein

By now you hopefully have a clearer – if not totally clear! – picture of your purpose and what it will take for you to realize your potential.

It is time to develop your goal process to fully live your passion and realize your potential – and we call it a goal *process* because that's exactly what it is.

It's more than just achieving the thing at the end. It's achieving through an entire process and growing and developing along the journey, just as you will have undoubtedly grown and developed along this one.

> *"We find no real satisfaction or happiness in life without obstacles to conquer and goals to achieve."* Maxwell Maltz

Consider...

QUESTION: Have you ever planned a holiday?

Chances are the answer is "yes".

NEXT QUESTION: Have you ever planned your life?

For many people the answer will be "no". So many of us just don't even consider that idea yet the benefits can be substantial.

In one of his sessions, Anthony Robbins mentions a study that was done where the graduating class at Yale University was interviewed about what they wanted to achieve in life.

Less than 3% of the class had a clear and specific set of goals and a plan for their achievement.

Twenty years later the surviving class members were interviewed and the 3% not only appeared happier and more well adjusted, they were worth more in financial terms than the other 97% **COMBINED**!

> *"You're not a failure if you don't make it. You're a success because you tried."* Susan Jeffers

The Plan + Emotion

"The reason most people never reach their goals is that they don't define them, or ever seriously consider them as believable or achievable. Winners can tell you where they are going, what they plan to do along the way, and who will be sharing the adventure with them." Denis Waitley

It's one thing to have your goals and another to support them with a written plan for their achievement.

Many people have heard of SMART goals:

S	=	Specific
M	=	Measurable
A	=	Achievable or Action-Oriented
R	=	Realistic or Results-Focused
T	=	Time-Related

This is an excellent start, though the one thing you are missing is **EMOTION!**

You need to FEEL IT!!! FEEL the EXCITEMENT!!!

Consider...

❑ Write down what you want to achieve and how do you want to feel?

❑ Ensure that it is in line with the SMART goals from above.

Consider...

- Next, consider enhancing even further the role of **emotion** in achieving your goal. What can you do to create an even more powerful emotional pull *toward* your goal and a powerful emotional push *away* from what you don't want?

- Then **SEE** yourself achieving that goal! Feel the excitement! Notice all the sights, sounds, smells... Visualize it in fine detail and **FEEL GREAT ABOUT IT!**

- What does it look like?

- What does it sound like?

- What does it smell like?

- What does it FEEL like?

- Finally, consider **habit**. What is one new habit that you can do every day, possibly even several times per day, to reinforce and assist you to achieve your goal and to successfully negotiate the goal process?

Review

It's time to call your Cheer Squad back in again!

Consider...

- ❏ Present your written goal and achievement plan to your Cheer Squad and ask them to review it in line with the following:
- ❏ Is it specific?
- ❏ Is it measurable?
- ❏ Is it achievable?
- ❏ Is it results-focused?
- ❏ Is it time-specific?
- ❏ Have you included creating new memories that support your goal?
- ❏ Have you included emotions that pull you toward what you want and push you away from what you don't?
- ❏ Have you included creating new habits that support your goal?
- ❏ Do you passionately want to achieve it???

Their comments:

Maybe the "how" is none of your business?

We have just spent quite some time looking at the role of planning in your goal setting and achieving process.

I have a question for you and something that at first glance may seem as though it is in opposition to the work we have just done.

What if the "how" is actually none of your business and totally out of our control?

There is a school of thought, to which I subscribe, that the achievement of our goals essentially has three parts:

1. Ask for what you want
2. God, The Universe or Divine Power (substitute whatever works for you) Answers
3. You Receive

If that is the case, why don't we have everything we want simply by asking?

There are many answers to this last question – here are a few:

❑   You are not clear about what you want
❑   You are not passionate enough in your resolve
❑   You don't 100% believe you can have it
❑   You just expect it to show up without taking any appropriate action
❑   You are not in a position where you are *ready* to receive the response
❑   You have spent so long working out every single step along the way, and dogmatically holding on to each step, there is no room for the Universe to bring to you what you require to achieve beyond your expectations.

Think about a time when you had a goal in mind, and you wanted this goal with all your heart, mind and soul.

Did things and people start to appear as if by magic who were able to help you toward your goal? People and things that you didn't even realize existed?

Consider...

❑ How can you be clearer about your goal?

❑ How can you increase the level of passion you have around your goal?

❑ How can you increase your level of certainty and faith that you will achieve your goal?

❑ How can you place yourself in a better position to receive the response(s) from the Universe?

Week 13: Realizing Your Potential

"Never look at the visible supply. Look always at the limitless riches in formless substance, and KNOW that they are coming to you as fast as you can receive and use them. Nobody, by cornering the visible supply, can prevent you from getting what is yours." - *Wallace D. Wattles*

"There are admirable potentialities in every human being. Believe in your strength and your youth. Learn to repeat endlessly to yourself, 'It all depends on me.'"Andre Gide

As we explored in the previous exercise, knowing the first steps is vital to being able to successfully navigate the change process and achieving your ultimate goal – living your passion and realizing your potential.

Other ingredients to consider are:

- ❑ Asking better questions to get better answers.
- ❑ Trying before you buy.
- ❑ Jumping right in.
- ❑ No such thing as failure.
- ❑ Where are you spending your time?

Asking Better Questions

"Asking questions is a very good way to find out about something." Kermit The Frog

- ❑ Why?
- ❑ What?
- ❑ When?
- ❑ Where?
- ❑ How?
- ❑ What if?
- ❑ Which one?

Learning to ask better questions will assist you enormously on your journey.

"Judge of a man by his questions rather than by his answers." Voltaire

Consider...

- ❑ If you don't already, start asking for clarification on things.
- ❑ Ask for more information on anything that you do not fully understand.

Taking Action!

> *"Man is by nature restless. When left too long in one place he will inevitably grow bored, unmotivated, and unproductive."* Ricardo Semler, Author of "Maverick"

It is one thing to go through the process of working out what you want to do with the rest of your life – including *today!* – and another thing to actually take ***action***.

All through this Journal you have been taking action in various forms.

You have been reviewing how you do what you do.

You have been searching within yourself for different answers.

You have been working continually toward the accomplishment of your goal – discovering your passion and realizing your potential.

Now, you need to summon up the courage to continue with that *action* because you are closer than ever to having everything you have ever dreamed of having in your life, and for some people this thought is scary enough to now *stop* them from taking action.

> *"Everything you want is out there waiting for you to ask. Everything you want also wants you. But you have to take action to get it."* Jack Canfield

Trying Before You Buy

Have you discovered your passion only to learn that it's something you have never really done before?

If so, consider trying it out before jumping in.

Or, maybe you have done it before however you are scared to passionately pursue it? If so, what about starting with something relatively simple?

"Never let the fear of striking out get in your way." George Herman "Babe" Ruth

Consider...

❑ Choose one area of your passion and volunteer or take a class. For example, if you want to be a writer and have never done any serious writing, consider taking a writing class.

Jumping Right In

"Take the first step in faith. You don't have to see the whole staircase, just take the first step." Dr. Martin Luther King Jr.

Just the opposite of the previous exercise, sometimes it is important to summon up the courage to dive in!

"Every artist was first an amateur." Ralph Waldo Emerson

Consider...

❑ Choose one area of your passion and find a way to dive straight in. For example, if you want to be a writer and have never done any serious writing, write an article and submit it to a newspaper or magazine that prints your subject matter.

No such thing as failure

During your journey there will be things that work out the way you want them to and things that don't.

The important element to remember is that there is no such thing as failure. Think of it this way: **Action produces Result**

The result may or may not be what you were hoping would happen, but regardless, it is simply a result. Next time, you might consider a different action in order to possibly bring about a different result.

Where are you spending your time?

Remember we discussed earlier in this journey about the fact that we all have the same amount of time?

We also looked at where you were spending your time – on problems or passions?

It is important at this point to demonstrate to yourself that your purpose is more important to you than your problems by dedicating your time in direct proportion to your priorities.

"Set priorities for your goals. A major part of successful living lies in the ability to put first things first. Indeed, the reason most major goals are not achieved is that we spend our time doing second things first." Robert J. McKain

Consider...

❑ Consider this: if you were to simply spend 5% **more** time on your purpose and 5% **less** time on your problems, what might you achieve?

Be Prepared For Success!

"Get a good idea and stay with it. Dog it, and work at it until it's done right." Walt Disney

---

As the quote from Walt Disney says, find something worthwhile and persist until you succeed.

"I find that the harder I work, the more luck I seem to have." Thomas Jefferson

---

Work hard at your passion and be prepared for the Universe to reward your efforts – some call this "luck".

"Happiness depends upon ourselves." Aristotle

Choose to be happy.

"We need men who can dream of things that never were." John F. Kennedy

---

Dream big dreams.

"The way our brain is wired up we only see what we believe is possible." Candice Pert

---

Believe that anything is possible.

"Few people know so clearly what they want. Most people can't even think what to hope for when they throw a penny in a fountain." Barbara Kingsolver, Animal Dreams

---

Even if you haven't been able to discover your purpose, know that you are further along than you were.

"That's the way things come clear. All of a sudden. And then you realize how obvious they've been all along." Madeleine L'Engle

Be prepared for the unexpected.

"God grant me the serenity to accept the things I cannot change, the courage to change the things I can, and the wisdom to know the difference." Reinhold Niebuhr

Accept that sometimes you may think you have discovered your passion only to find that things have changed – or that *you* have changed.

"Life is either a daring adventure or nothing." Helen Keller

Be daring, take risks and **have the adventure of your life**!

168

Final Words

"There came a time when the risk to remain tight in the bud was more painful than the risk it took to blossom."
Anaïs Nin

Discovering what you want to be is often not an easy process – if it were, everyone would know what they want to be! Equally, realizing your potential is not an easy process – if it were, we would all be achieving great things.

"The greatest discovery of my generation is that a human being can alter his life by altering his attitude."
William James

The reality is that it may take some hard work; it takes introspection; it takes critical thinking; and above all it takes the courage to take the risks to make it all happen.

There will be people who will be on your side and "dream-stealers" who will tell you every reason why your passion is ridiculous.

"Nothing will ever be attempted if all possible objections must first be overcome." *Samuel Johnson*

You will be your own worst critic.

"Don't bother just to be better than your contemporaries or predecessors. Try to be better than yourself." *William Faulkner*

Remember, you really can be all you ever dreamed of being!

I would like to leave you with a quote by Michael Landon that I hope will inspire you to be all you can be and to do it now.

"Someone should tell us, right at the start of our lives, that we are dying. Then we might live life to the limit, every minute of every day.
Do it, I say! Whatever you want to do, do it now!
There are only so many tomorrows."
Michael Landon

"If you can DREAM it, you can DO it." Walt Disney

Your Thoughts…

About the Author

www.LeighStJohn.com

Widely acknowledged as an Achievement Strategist (personal, professional and organizational achievement), Leigh is a respected Corporate Facilitator, Host/MC, Media Presenter, Speaker and Author whose purpose is to help people realize their potential and inspire them to take action.

An accomplished entrepreneur in her own right, she owns and has owned a wide range of businesses from hairdressing to publishing to photography and more... all geared to helping people "shine" from the inside out.

Leigh's achievements also include being the International Ambassador & Spokesperson for "Silence" - breaking the 'silence' of child sexual abuse (World Premiere at Cannes International Film Festival 2006); Drive Time Co-Host with a major commercial radio station; a Daily Columnist with a major regional newspaper: *'Life with Leigh'*; Australian Ambassador to the International Virtual Women's Chamber of Commerce; Managing Editor of *Achievers' Magazine*; Expert Columnist for *Dynamic Small Business Magazine*; Weekly Writer for the American Magazine, *Premyier*; Sponsor and Mentor for the Secondary Schools' Australian Business Week and a Member of various Commonwealth New Enterprise Incentive Scheme (NEIS) Advisory Committees.

In addition to the corporate sector, Leigh has managed charities in both the USA and Australia, spent many years working with disadvantaged groups such as those who are long-term unemployed as well as working specifically with disadvantaged women, youth and with women in small business.

Leigh has qualifications in Journalism, Non-Profit Management and Adult Education; has studied Psychology, Marketing and Communications; is licensed with the Commission for Children and Young People; is a Telstra Business Woman of the Year Award nominee (Australia's leading business women's award) and a Finalist in the International Women's Day Leadership Awards.

Always one to try new things, Leigh has flown an aeroplane, performed as a vocalist and soloist ranging from classical to contemporary and jazz, driven in a celebrity speedway race, won prizes for her artwork and writing, established several businesses and much more...

A survivor of ten years of abuse while growing up, then a life-threatening illness, followed by living with an auto-immune disease that Leigh says "sometimes slowed me down but never stopped me", Leigh St John is a practical example of the Aussie spirit of relaxed achievement.

Referred to as an 'Achievement Guru' by ABC, Leigh has worked with some of the world's top companies; written several books and hundreds of articles; is a Rotary Centurion; a Member of Mensa; the Variety Club; and the Panel of Professional Advisers for the Victorian Government.

On a personal note...

From Leigh: At my core, I am someone who loves to smile and to make others smile - and someone who gets a thrill beyond words when I can truly help someone to see their own potential, increase their confidence and "shine"!

I have faith in the power of the human spirit and that we each have the ability to achieve whatever we believe in and anything upon which we focus our intention and actions!

Although my early years contained a great deal of sadness with the death of my father when I was six years old; and years of abuse that followed; I had the amazing gift of having my great-grandmother as my role model and mentor - a wonderful woman born just after the end of the 1800's. I learned when to wear gloves, when to wear a hat, how to whittle my own pegs, to wash clothes with a wash-board (very useful in today's society!), and how to be at ease in any situation – and help others feel at ease – whether at a casual BBQ or at a formal occasion meeting Royalty.

Nan taught me to be respectful of all people, no matter what they do for a living, the colour of their skin, the religious doctrine they follow, or how much is in their bank account; to remain positive (she was the first to nickname me Pollyanna); and to always look for the beauty in everyone and everything. I cannot thank her enough for the wonderful insights she brought to my life and I would like to think that she is proud of the person I have become.

I love technology, audio and video editing, developing websites, streaming media, and 'playing' with gadgets and gizmos. Referred to as "crazy" by some friends, I actually find that kind of thing more like a hobby than work – it's fun! (ok, so maybe my friends are right! ☺)

I am passionate about providing resources and avenues to assist people and organizations to truly 'shine' and this passion is at the core of each of my personal and professional endeavours.

I believe Gratitude and Love are among the most powerful forces in the Universe – and when combined with unwavering faith, allow you to achieve your heart's desire.

Someone once asked me what I would like to have people think of me after I have left this dimension and hopefully moved on to the next. I have since thought about that question and my answer is this:

"I hope that I have made people smile and that in some small way I have helped them to realize that they have **unlimited** potential; and assisted and inspired them increase their confidence and discover the strategies they need to realize that potential and "shine".

With faith, focus and determined action, anything truly is possible!"

I would love to hear from you and for you to share the impossible that _you_ made possible!

You can find my contact information at: **www.LeighStJohn.com**

Thank you for allowing me to have been part of your journey.

With love and gratitude,

Leigh St John

How do you know when you have found your Purpose?

Without doubt, one of the best explanations I have heard for what it is like when you find your purpose is an excerpt from *Wink and Grow Rich* by Roger Hamilton:

"When you find your vision, everything will suddenly become crystal clear. You will look around and say, "So THAT'S what the world is supposed to look like!" That is when you will be begin to attract the people, the opportunities and the wealth you desire."

*My wish for you is that you become so clear, so motivated, so inspired and so **alive** that there is no doubt – **you have discovered what you want to be!***

Other suggested study:

Throughout this book we have relied on the inspirational and thought-provoking quotations of others.

You will find this list of quotes and others at www.LeighStJohn.com

I suggest taking these quotes – either in turn or simply the ones that appeal to your heart and spirit – and learning more about the author of the quote.

Who are/were they?

What did they accomplish?

What challenges did the overcome in their life?

What can you learn from them?

Additionally, please feel free to contact me via www.LeighStJohn.com for other resources or potential speaking engagements and workshops.

Have fun!

Your Thoughts…

CPSIA information can be obtained at www.ICGtesting.com
Printed in the USA
BVOW030251301211

279490BV00005B/85/P